Is there Death in the Pot?

Replacement Theology Exposed

18/5/12
To Les,
With much love
in Jesus,
from Frank
(the author)

Rev. Frank Andrews M.Div. B.Ed. (Hons)

Is there Death in the Pot?

Onwards and Upwards Publications, Berkeley House,
11 Nightingale Crescent, West Horsley, Surrey KT24 6PD

www.onwardsandupwards.org

copyright © Rev. Frank Andrews 2012

The right of Rev. Frank Andrews to be identified as the author of this work has been asserted by the author in accordance with the Copyright, Designs and Patents Act 1988.

All rights reserved.

No part of this publication may be reproduced or transmitted in any form or by any means, electronic or mechanical, including photocopy, recording or any information storage and retrieval system, without permission in writing from the author or publisher.

Scripture quotations are taken from the Holy Bible, NEW INTERNATIONAL VERSION © 1978, 1984 by International Bible Society. Used by permission of Hodder & Stoughton. All rights reserved.

ISBN: 978-1-907509-42-1
Cover design: Leah-Maarit

Printed in the UK

Dedication

I wish to dedicate this book to my parents, Frank Andrews (Snr) and the late Joyce Andrews. They have always been a great inspiration to me.

I also dedicate my book to the late Russell Cohen, who taught me so much about Jewish life and culture and to the members of the fellowship, which have been faithful to the Lord and to me over the years.

Endorsements

This book deserves to be widely read by all those who want to know the truth. I hope it will encourage many to discover what the Bible *really* says about God's purposes for the Jew, the Gentile and Israel.

Elise Hedger
Co-ordinator for Third Name Link

It has been my privilege to be taught by Pastor Frank Andrews over the last nine years. Pastor Frank has a passion for biblical truth and contending for the faith once delivered to the saints. He is dedicated to God's call upon his life to see the Church restored to its Hebraic roots. I would encourage every believer to read this book with an open heart.

Mary Duckworth
Member of the leadership team
Hyndburn Christian Fellowship

I joined Pastor Andrews' fellowship about three months after my conversion. During the first 'Prayer for Israel' meeting which I attended with other members of the fellowship, I was touched by the message which Pastor gave that night. I asked God to give me his love for the Jewish people. That love for the Jewish people has grown in my heart since that day over seven years ago. I have constantly been built up through Pastor's excellent teaching ministry. I believe Pastor's book exposing Replacement Theology is simple and to the point, arising from his passion to see biblical truths restored to the wider Church. My prayer is that all who read it may come to know the debt that we as Gentiles owe to the dear Jewish people.
God bless you.

Carl Taylor
Treasurer / member of the leadership team
Hyndburn Christian Fellowship

Contents

About the Author

Frank Andrews became a Christian at the age of thirteen through the ministry of the Christian Union at his secondary school.

Trained to teach secondary age students, he specialized in Theology and History and was awarded B.Ed(Hons). Frank taught for twenty-two years in secondary schools both in England and Zimbabwe. He was Head of History at Oriel Boys' School in Harare Zimbabwe and Head of Religious Education at North Manchester High School for Boys.

In 1990 he was ordained as Pastor in the Assemblies of God Church in Zimbabwe. After completing his probationary period in ministry, he pioneered a new branch of the fellowship in the southern suburbs of Harare. He went on to establish Hyndburn Christian Fellowship in the area of Accrington and was recognized by the Multiply Christian Network as a minister of Religion in the U.K.

In 2004 Frank had a serious stroke, causing him to retire from teaching in the education sector. Having enjoyed a reasonable degree of healing (but still dependent upon God to overcome his disabilities) he undertook further theological study through different theological institutions, culminating in his award of Master of Divinity.

Frank has always had a love and respect for the Jewish people from the time of his conversion. Over time he has recognized the call of God to serve Him by exposing the error of Replacement Theology and highlighting the appalling consequences, the fruit of this doctrine, through the centuries of Church History.

Foreword by Dr. Howard Morgan

Pastor Frank Andrews' book 'Is There Poison in the Pot?' is a welcome source of information exposing and refuting the demonic doctrine of Replacement Theology. Written in a succinct and clear way, this book will prove to be a valuable introduction to this subject which has brought so much corruption to the Body of Christ and evil and suffering to the Jewish people. Those who read it and continue to study will find this book a spiritual weapon that the Holy Spirit can use in their battle against the twin demonic principalities of Anti-Semitism and Anti-Christ.

The spiritual poison of Replacement Theology has been one of the historic tactics of the devil to remove the Church from her Jewish roots and distort and then destroy her biblical relationship and responsibility to love and testify to the Jewish people about their own Messiah. With the goal of causing the Church to be the enemy of the Jews, in direct opposition to God's call upon the Body of Christ to be a loving witness to Israel of her Messiah, these two demonic principalities continue in their deluded attempts to hinder the present purposes of God from being fulfilled, believing they can nullify God's prophetic promises concerning the Jewish people, the Land of Israel, the City of Jerusalem, the Temple Mount, and the return of the Jewish Messiah Yeshua.

Replacement Theology is one of those attempts, but God has raised up ministers like Pastor Andrews, who exposes this poison and explains that the antidote is for believers to receive God's heart and the truths of His eternal Word concerning the relationship between the Church and the Jewish people.

I pray that as you read this important book you will be inspired and equipped to be part of the 'antidote' to this poisonous, demonic teaching that has infected so many within Christendom.

Dr Howard Morgan
Author of 'For Zion's Sake'.

Introduction

What is Replacement Theology?

Let me begin this introduction by explaining my choice of book title. "There is death in the pot" were the words spoken to the prophet Elisha by the sons of the prophets. These were words of great sorrow regarding the only pot of food that these men had to eat to quench their great hunger in the days of a great famine that had struck the land of Israel. The whole story is recounted to us in 2 Kings 4:38-41. This story had a happy ending. Elisha spoke the word of the Lord, which they obeyed. As soon as they put a handful of meal into the pot the poison was neutralised and everyone could eat of its contents. I believe that the doctrine of Replacement Theology is like that poison in the pot. This poison has entered the Christian church largely because of an ignorance of the meaning of certain biblical passages. Some good people sadly got things badly wrong. The source of this error obviously involved Gentile Church leaders becoming proud that they had taken over the running of the church from the Jewish leaders who had worked together to establish it. Like the poison in the pot during the days of Elisha, this poisonous doctrine has brought tremendous suffering to Jesus' natural brethren, the Jewish people. On many occasions it has led to the death of innocent Jewish people. Furthermore, I believe that the doctrine of Replacement Theology has brought a large measure of spiritual death to the Church. I also believe it has brought intense pain and sorrow to the heart of God himself. All these issues will be explored throughout the pages of this book.

Replacement Theology is a relatively new title used to describe a very old doctrinal belief. The old title of this doctrine was *Supersessionism*. Many theologians still use this title when attempting to defend the beliefs of those who believe that the Church has become the new 'chosen people' which has replaced the Jews in the plan of God. They suggest that the Church has superseded Israel. All the biblical promises which prior to Jesus' coming applied to Israel now apply to the Church. Theologians who believe in supersessionism are divided into two camps. Those that believe in *economic supersessionism* hold that following Jesus' coming as Messiah of Israel her mission had been completed. They believe that the Church alone is the vehicle through which God fulfils his purpose of redemption in the world. Those that believe in *punitive supersessionism* hold that Israel has been punished for rejecting Jesus, her Messiah. God's punishment for this rejection is that God has chosen the Church to be the New Israel. The Church alone now fulfils God's purpose of redemption in the world. Many theologians belonging to this school of thought have actually suggested that the Jews are all cursed for killing Christ. Theologians that believe in the concept of supersessionism suggest that the restoration of the State of Israel in 1948 was a quirk of history rather than a fulfilment of biblical prophecy. They believe that all biblical prophecies regarding Israel's restoration to her land should be spiritualised and applied to the Church. One of the major defenders of the doctrine of Replacement Theology is Bruce Waltke. He wrote:

> *The Jewish nation no longer has a place as the special people of God; that place has been taken over by the Christian community which fulfils God's purpose for Israel.*[1]

Dr Gary Hendrick, in his article 'Replacement Theology, its Origins, Teaching and Errors' has written much regarding the negative impact of Replacement Theology upon the Church. He has written:

> *Is Replacement Theology really worth arguing about? Or is this discussion much ado about nothing? One reason it's important to call attention to questionable theology, no matter how deeply entrenched it might be in traditional Christianity, is that sooner or later, bad theology always leads to bad practice. In this case this bad theology has already led to bad practice. Replacement Theology has provided the basis of all sorts of mischief, persecution and atrocities against the Jewish people throughout Christian history.*[2]

---

[1] *Continuity and Discontinuity: Perspectives on the Testaments*, edited by John Feinberg, p 275
[2] *Replacement Theology, its Origins, Teaching and Errors*, Dr Gary Hendrick

In simple terms then most adherents of Replacement Theology believe that God has rejected the Jewish people from their role as the 'chosen people' due to their rejection of Jesus, their true Messiah. Many supporters of this doctrine go further than this in their condemnation of all Jews, labelling them as 'Christ-killers'.

They suggest that when the Jewish crowd at Pilate's judgement seat asked that his blood be upon them and their children that God enacted this curse upon them. They claim that the blood guilt is permanently upon all Jews as a result of their being to blame for Jesus' death. The only way for them to be free of God's curse is to repent and embrace both the faith and culture of Christianity. They must, in effect, repent of all that is Jewish about them. Supporters of Replacement Theology claim that all the feasts celebrated by the Jewish community should not be celebrated by Christians despite the fact that God himself actually commissioned these feasts. Many of these supporters seem completely ignorant of the fact that Holy Communion itself arose out of the Passover meal that Jesus celebrated with his disciples as their last supper together before he faced the terrible ordeal of the cross. They seem totally unaware that Jesus used the symbols that had been present on the Passover table to establish the communion as the central ritual which most Christians regularly engage in today.

On a rather amusing note I will share with you a peculiar incident that occurred one Christmas time when I was presiding at a Communion Service after returning from my stay in Zimbabwe as an ordained Minister of Religion. To my surprise on the table there was a currant bun with white icing on top in the place where the unleavened bread should have been. When I pointed out to one of the church officers that I was not willing to ask that God should bless this symbol as representing the body of our Lord Jesus, he was completely amazed by my response. He protested claiming that this church had always done this at Christmas. When I continued in my protest, explaining that we should use unleavened bread if it was available (since this is symbolic of the fact that Jesus was and is the sinless sacrifice for our sin), he reluctantly relented and brought out the unleavened bread. I don't think this church officer ever forgave me for going against his little Christmas treat for the congregation. If this church leader had been aware of the origin of the communion in the context of the Jewish Passover Meal he would never have made this mistake.

One of the major beliefs of those who support Replacement Theology is that God has replaced the Jewish people by embracing the Gentile Church as his new chosen people. The Church, they claim, has produced much better fruit than the nation of Israel. I find this an incredible claim to make once one starts to study church history in any depth. Obviously there are some shining lights in the dark history of Christianity. However, these shining lights do not out-shine the sad darkness of the corruption of church leaders and the violent actions of one group of Christians persecuting their fellow Christians simply because they differ in their beliefs as to how the Bible should be interpreted. Any person studying church history will be also saddened by the terrible acts of persecution launched against members of other religions, especially Jews and Muslims, in the name of Jesus, who taught his followers to love their enemies. (See Matthew 5:43-48). On the positive side, Christians have worked together to end slavery, improve mining and factory conditions, and to bring education and medical treatment to people around the world.

In the light of these facts, I believe that we Christians cannot claim to be a 'chosen people' due to our good works and faithfulness in producing good fruit. I believe that it is by God's grace that we become acceptable to him as individuals by accepting his undeserved mercy and love towards us. It was because of God's mercy and love towards us that Jesus laid down his life upon the cross for us. No one could take the life of Jesus; he laid down his life in order to set us free from the power of sin. (See John 10:17-18). The apostle Paul made it very clear to the church at Ephesus that all believers in Jesus are saved because of the grace of God, not because of any good works that they may have done. (See Ephesians 2:8-10). I believe that this principle regarding the grace of God applies also to his appointing Israel to be a 'chosen people' and his appointing the Church to be alongside them as a 'chosen people'. Israel became a chosen people not because they had earned God's election but rather due solely to the grace of God. In the same way, I believe, God appointed the Church to be a chosen people due to his grace. God foreknew that many times his

Church would let him down. The Church, like Israel, would also fail to produce consistently good fruit. I believe that Apostle Paul made it clear to the church at Rome in his letter to them that the Gentiles would never replace the Jewish people as a chosen people. (See Romans 11:1-6, 17-26). In this chapter Paul pointed out to the Gentiles (non-Jews) in the Church at Rome that they should never become boastful over the fact that God had grafted them into the natural olive tree (representing the believing, faithful Jewish community). He warned them that because the wild olive branches were grafted into the cultivated tree they should be careful not to be boastful. If they became boastful God could remove them again.

It is apparent from church history that the Gentile believers in Jesus have consistently ignored this warning from the apostle Paul. Replacement Theology arises from a terrible arrogance on the part of Gentile believers in Jesus. They are, in effect, doing the thing Paul urged them not to do: boasting about themselves as being better than the Jews. I believe Jesus' words to the Samaritan woman in John 4:22 are a constant reminder of the debt that we as his followers owe to the Jewish people. Jesus said, "Salvation is of the Jews."

How can we fail to acknowledge the debt we owe to the faithful Jewish people who risked their very lives to bring the gospel to us as Gentile Christians? Indeed, we should also remember the Jews who sacrificed their lives for the sake of fulfilling Jesus' commission to take the gospel out to the whole world. We also should remember the fact that the entire Bible is a Jewish book. All of the books it contains, with the exception of three, were written by Jewish authors.

Throughout the rest of my book I will demonstrate my belief that Replacement Theology is completely unscriptural and contrary in every way to the teaching of our Lord Jesus. I will also seek to expose the dreadful things that have taken place throughout Church history simply because those who have professed to follow the teaching of Jesus have believed in this poisonous doctrine. Moreover, I will seek to explore some of the historical factors which have influenced prominent church leaders to believe in, and to teach their followers, the doctrine of Replacement Theology.

The aim of my book is not only to better inform Christians in regard to the issues that I will put forward but also, by the grace of God, to help us as believers in Jesus to develop a love for the Jewish people. My hope is that readers of this book will cultivate the fruit of the Holy Spirit in regard to humility. When we share the gospel, may we always do it with patience and be motivated by the love of God. In particular, my prayer is that we should all be enabled by God to share with the Jewish people the 'good news' concerning their Messiah in humility and with sensitivity. I believe we can only do this when we understand how anti-Jewishness and its consequences have affected Jews over the centuries.

Supposing for one moment that the advocates of Replacement Theology have a sound basis in regard to the teaching of the New Testament, one would expect to find that Jesus himself would, to some extent, repudiate his own Jewishness. As we shall observe in the next chapter this was certainly not the case. Jesus celebrated his Jewishness. He concentrated on his fellow Jews, preparing them to spread the gospel to everyone across the Roman Empire. Again, if Replacement Theology has a sound biblical basis one would expect the early church to have had extremely little success among the Jews and to have had to quickly turn to the Gentiles to achieve any degree of success. In fact, as we shall observe in my chapter reviewing the history of the early church, the opposite was true. The early church had an amazing degree of success in recruiting thousands of ordinary Jews into its ranks and even a large degree of success in recruiting Jewish religious leaders into its ranks.

When I started my research regarding the topics I would cover in this book, I never realised the extent of the division of opinion among evangelical Christians that exists over the issue of how the Church should relate to the Jewish people and the State of Israel. Underlying this serious debate among Christians is the doctrine of Replacement Theology. Modern advocates of this doctrine are inclined to be vehemently opposed to the very existence of the State of Israel. They perceive the creation of the State of Israel as an historical accident which has nothing at all to do with the fulfilment of biblical prophecy or the providence of God. Some of these advocates of Replacement Theology go much further than this and perceive the State of Israel as a fundamentally racist institution worthy of their condemnation. Dr. Stephen Sizer, a prominent advocate of Replacement Theology, has stated on his website:

'In 1975, the United Nations General Assembly passed Resolution 3379 defining Zionism as "a form of racism and racial discrimination". Contemporary Christian Zionism is in part a reaction to increasing world-wide criticism of Israel's form of apartheid.'

What he fails to state is that the United Nations rarely acts in an ethical manner. It is composed of nations that act upon what they perceive as their national self-interest. Little wonder then that most nations are willing to dance to the tune of the oil-rich Arab nations upon whom they depend economically. He also conveniently fails to consider the fact that the State of Israel, when it was formed, offered all the Arabs living within their borders the full rights of citizenship. The group of Arabs, now called Palestinians, refused this generous offer and went into voluntary exile. Those Arabs who chose to remain in the newly formed State of Israel have been granted equality of rights with the Jewish people. I would suggest that these are not the actions of a racist, apartheid state. I will return to this theme later. The advocates of Replacement Theology believe that they are the voice of ethical Christianity, speaking out for the human rights of the oppressed Palestinians. I am particularly indebted to the work of Dr. Paul Wilkinson regarding the evolution of many of the advocates of Replacement Theology into a very active and vocal pro-Palestinian lobby. His article on this relatively new trend, which he calls *Christian Palestinianism*, has both informed me and inspired me to undertake further research regarding this phenomenon. Christians who believe that Replacement Theology is fundamentally wrong and that the rebirth of the State of Israel in 1948 was the fulfilment of biblical prophecy are referred to as Christian Zionists. I am pleased to belong to this group of Christian believers.

The debate among Christians over the issue of Replacement Theology is of vital importance to the life of the Church. If the modern advocates of Replacement Theology are right, Christian Zionists are fundamentally wrong, and we are acting as the unwitting instruments of racism, contrary to God's will and purposes. If the modern advocates of Replacement Theology are wrong they are deceived by a poisonous doctrine and are working contrary to God's will and purposes. That is not to say that I doubt the sincerity of the motives of these men and women. They believe that they are fulfilling God's will regarding upholding and defending the rights of the Palestinians, an ethnic group which they believe has been oppressed by the Israelis. This issue is of vital importance given that, rightly or wrongly, Israel is battling for its right to exist and the conflict between the State of Israel and the Palestinians is never far from the top of the world's news agenda. We should all remember that one day we, as Christian believers, will give an account to God of how we have lived our lives. (See Romans 14:10-12). I am certain that how we have related to the Jewish people as an ethnic group and how we have responded to the Israeli-Palestinian issue will be part of God's agenda that we will need to respond to. Teachers of biblical truths need to be very conscious of the fact that we will be held even more accountable for the content of the things we teach. (See James 3:1). The issues which are addressed in this book are, therefore, issues of vital significance. They are not just of interest and relevance to church ministers and trainee ministers. They are surely of interest and relevance to all Christians. With this in mind, I have endeavoured to explain the theological terms and concepts used in this book in a relatively simple manner.

The Jewishness of Jesus

All books regarding Christianity rightly focus upon our Saviour Jesus, whom the Bible calls "the author and finisher of our faith". The issue of the Jewishness of Jesus is for me, and I believe for all his followers, an absolutely vital issue. As this book will reveal, there has been a sad history regarding the relationship between the Christian church and the Jewish community. It seems almost unbelievable that those who have professed to be followers of Jesus have committed terrible acts of cruelty and violence against his natural brethren. Had these believers in Jesus understood the fact that Jesus was, is and will always be Jewish, they would surely never have engaged in these dreadful acts in his name. The wonderful truth of the incarnation is that Jesus will always remain perfectly God and perfectly man. Historic Christianity has always confessed that Jesus took upon himself our humanity on a permanent basis. This is the view of all the New Testament authors. Since Jesus was undoubtedly born of the Virgin Mary, a young Jewish lady, this obviously makes Jesus a member of the Jewish race.

The Gospel of Luke makes it clear that Jesus' parents presented him at the Temple in Jerusalem to make the appropriate sacrifice for his birth and had their son circumcised according to the Law of Moses. Jesus is presented as regularly attending the synagogue on the Jewish Sabbath Day (Luke 4:15-16). Luke clearly implies that Jesus found widespread acceptance of his teaching in many of the synagogues of Galilee during his early ministry. The only exception to this was when Jesus visited the synagogue in his native Nazareth where he grew up.

When Jesus was tempted by the devil he answered each temptation by the appropriate use of the Old Testament - the Jewish Scriptures which he knew so well. Jesus' twelve disciples were clearly all Jewish. Indeed all the writers of the New Testament were Jewish with the one exception of Luke. However, Luke himself drew all the information he used to write both his gospel and the Acts of the Apostles from the Jewish eyewitnesses of Jesus' ministry and the expansion of the early church. The facts I am referring to seem obvious. However, not all Christians seem to be aware of these facts.

One funny incident a Jewish friend of mine experienced sadly illustrates the lack of understanding some Christians have in regard to the details regarding Jesus' ministry. My friend was approached by a Pentecostal Christian who was attempting to share her faith with her. The Christian lady asked my friend if she was Jewish and if she was on her way home from "one of those synagogues". When she told her that this was the case, the Christian lady suggested that the Jews were to blame for the death of Jesus and that due to this they had now been rejected by God. She went so far as to say that the Jews are now cursed by God. Perhaps the Christian lady would have benefitted greatly from a course entitled 'How to win friends and influence people'. She was completely shocked when my Jewish friend quoted the New Testament in response to her.

She asked, "Are not all people to blame for the death of Jesus since we are all sinners and Jesus died for the sins of all mankind?" She then quoted Romans 3:23 to prove her point. "St. Paul wrote, 'For all have sinned and fallen short of the glory of God.'"

The Christian lady was amazed that she should know any part of the New Testament. She looked completely shocked. After a short pause she remarked, "How come you know passages from the New Testament?"

My friend quickly reminded her that the whole New Testament, with the exception of Luke's Gospel and the Acts of the Apostles was written by Jews.

Her reply revealed her ignorance in the matter. She said, "I never knew that."

Then my dear Jewish friend shocked her even more when she asked her if she had ever read the words of Jesus in John 10:17-18. She quoted Jesus' words stating that no one was able to take his life from him but that he was willing to lay it down and take it back up again.

The Christian lady had by now completely run out of steam, amazed at the biblical knowledge my friend had so clearly demonstrated. My friend then revealed the fact that many Jews are now Messianic, that they do believe that Jesus was and is the true Messiah of Israel and, indeed, the saviour of all mankind. She went on to reveal the fact that although she still went to synagogue on special occasions with her husband, she regularly attended church as well. Mystified, the Christian lady asked if she was one of those Messianic Jews she had spoken about. My friend confessed that indeed she was and is a follower of Jesus. She went on to explain how her husband, a very liberal Jew, never tried to stop her quietly attending church. She also explained that her husband had been called out to help with a medical emergency, leaving her to take their young children home after the synagogue service. At this point my friend gave her apologies and explained that she really needed to get the children home for lunch.

I imagine the elderly Pentecostal Christian never forgot this meeting. I wonder if she ever questioned why after so many years of attending a Christian Church she was so ignorant in regard to the Jewish origins of her faith in Jesus. I also wonder if she ever questioned after so many years of attending church (for she had confessed that she had received new birth as a teenager) that she could be so wrong in blaming the Jews for Jesus' death.

Sadly this amusing story reveals the fact that many Christians have misunderstood the fact that no one group can be blamed for killing Jesus. Throughout history Jews have been called 'Christ-killers' by those who have professed to be Christians. Helen Shapiro, a prominent Messianic singer and speaker, recounts how, as a young child, she was brought to tears when some Christian children called her a Christ-killer. She ran home in tears asking her mum if she was really to blame for the death of Christ.

Christians have not been helped to understand the fact that both Jesus and his disciples were Jewish by the way that Jesus has been represented by artists. Pictures of him as a young child with his virgin mother too often represent him as very English or Italian looking. Too often Jesus is represented as having blond hair and blue eyes. Christian art has too often shown a distorted picture of the scene of the Last Supper, with Jesus and the eleven disciples at the table looking very English. Only Judas, the traitor, is represented with obviously Jewish traits as darker-skinned with a larger hooked nose. He is often seen holding on tightly to his money bag. This puts across the wrong stereotype that all Jews are greedy and hold on tightly to their wealth.

Jesus' words, according to John's Gospel, clearly point to the fact that he rejoiced in his Jewishness and saw his fellow Jews as the means through which God would bring the knowledge of his salvation to all mankind. According to John 4:21-23, Jesus told the Samaritan woman that a time would come when people would no longer travel to worship God at the Samaritan temple or the Jewish temple; rather they would worship God in Spirit and in truth. Here Jesus clearly prophesied the destruction of the Temple in Jerusalem.

For this reason this particular passage is fairly well known. What is not so well known is that Jesus told the Samaritan that her people worshipped God without a true knowledge of him. The Jews however, Jesus told her, worshipped the True God according to a correct knowledge of him. Jesus went even further in his words to her. He said, "Salvation is of the Jews." I believe these words are very significant. I believe Jesus was clearly indicating the fact that it would be through his own Jewish race that God would take the gospel to the entire known world within the short time of a few decades. In order to do this, Jesus' Jewish followers would risk their lives, and many would even have to lay down their lives. In response to this fact, I believe we Gentile (non-Jewish) followers of Jesus owe a debt of respect and honour to the Jewish People.

All four Gospels clearly portray Jesus as attending God's Feasts which were given to Israel. In John chapter 7 Jesus is shown to have gone up to Jerusalem to celebrate the Feast of Tabernacles. Luke makes it clear that the Passover meal was the last supper that Jesus had with his disciples. (See Luke 22:1-8). It was at this meal, of course, that Jesus set up the symbols of the communion to represent his sacrifice upon the cross for us. It was undoubtedly the unleavened bread that Jesus used to represent his body. The unleavened bread can be seen as symbolic of Jesus having never committed sin.

Matthew shows Jesus sending his disciples to go to the lost sheep of the house of Israel (10:5-6). Jesus obviously wanted the mission to his fellow Jews to be completed before his disciples were sent out to all the nations. Jesus was widely accepted as a great rabbi by many ordinary Jewish men and women who came together in crowds to listen to his teaching and to see his miracles. He was so popular with his ordinary Jewish followers that the corrupt religious leaders had to plot to have Jesus arrested at night, fearing that his arrest during daylight hours might lead to a riot. That is why these religious leaders had to pay Judas thirty pieces of silver so that they might be able to have Jesus arrested at night. Thirty pieces of silver was a large amount of money to have to pay Judas for his betrayal of Jesus. It represented the amount of pay a Jewish labourer would have received for a whole year's work.

Even Nicodemus, a senior Pharisee who belonged to the Jewish religious council, came to see Jesus privately and called him 'Rabbi' meaning 'a teacher sent by God'. (See John 3). Not for one minute did Jesus question the sincerity of Nicodemus. He never labelled him a hypocrite. Jesus simply challenged him with the importance of the work that the Holy Spirit would do in his life when he was willing for this to take place. Later John portrays Nicodemus as identifying himself clearly as a follower of Jesus after his death upon the cross. He joined Joseph of Arimathea in assisting with the burial of Jesus. After this it was most unlikely that either man would have been permitted to remain as members of the Sanhedrin (the council which governed the religious affairs of the Jewish People).

The question now arises as to why Jesus should be thought by some as being opposed to his own people. This problem only arises when people confuse Jesus' opposition to many of the morally corrupt, hypocritical religious leaders with his supposed opposition to the Jews as a whole. In Matthew chapter 23 Jesus so clearly condemns the hypocrisy of the scribes and the Pharisees. These two groups of men were responsible for leading and directing the worship of God in the synagogues. The scribes were the rabbis, the teachers of the Jewish faith; the Pharisees acted like governing committees assisting them in governing the synagogues.

Jesus' main issue with them was that they completely failed to let love for God and their fellow men and women become the motivating factor behind all their religious duties. Instead pride, love of men's praise, love of their position in the religious hierarchy and love of wealth had become the motivating factors behind the performance of their religious duties. In theory, both Jesus and the rabbis of his day would have agreed on what the most important commandments of the Jewish Scriptures were. (See Mark 12:28-34). The most important commandment was to love God with all your heart, with all your soul, with all of your mind and all your strength. The second most important was to love your neighbour as yourself. The sad thing was that so many of the religious leaders of Jesus' day failed to let obeying these two most important commandments be the governing factor that determined how they would conduct all their religious duties and responsibilities.

Sadly, as we shall see later in my book, many Christian leaders have failed to let love for God and their fellow men and women be the governing factor as to how they have conducted their religious duties and responsibilities. This is a challenge to all of us as Christians: is love for God and our fellow human beings the motivation for all that we say and do? I am sure that if we give an honest answer to this question we will all realise just how much we too need the help of the Holy Spirit to make our lives more like Jesus. We too are in constant need of God's grace and forgiveness for the many times we fall short of living the kind of lives we are called to live, constantly motivated by our love for God and our neighbours, whoever they may be.

In a later chapter I will examine the conflict between Jesus and many of the Jewish religious leaders in greater depth. Whatever the differences between Jesus and these religious leaders, it is most clear that Jesus was widely accepted by the ordinary Jewish people. Even the religious leaders were divided among themselves over the issue of either backing or rejecting the ministry and teaching of Jesus. Some greatly admired him and even invited him to speak in their synagogues. They were impressed by his miracles, which they saw as a proof that God was confirming the validity of his teaching and ministry. Others opposed him strongly, even to the point of seeking to arrange his death.

What can certainly be said, having looked at the evidence relating to the Jewishness of Jesus found in the four Gospels, is that Jesus was and is Jewish. He enjoyed widespread acceptance among many of his people. Jesus obviously proclaimed the message that he was the fulfilment of the Jewish scriptures. He claimed to be the promised Messiah. He formed his Church among the Jewish people and commissioned them to proclaim the 'gospel' concerning him to the people of all nations.

The Jewishness of the Early Church

The history of the early church is laid out clearly for us in the Acts of the Apostles. There is no doubt that Luke, the Gentile doctor who travelled with Apostle Paul, is the author of this book. The information that Luke provides for us in this book is supplemented by the information given in the letters written by Paul, Peter, James, John and the author of the letter to the Hebrews.

Acts 1:8 suggests that Jesus set out a plan for proclaiming the good news regarding him to Jerusalem and Judea first, then to the Samaritans and to the Gentiles throughout the whole world. His disciples are shown in the Book of Acts to have followed this plan as they proclaimed to others that Jesus was, and is, the saviour of mankind. The first nine chapters of the Book of Acts show the disciples, now called 'the apostles' (meaning 'those who are sent by Jesus and by his authority'), first of all proclaiming their message to their fellow Jews in Jerusalem and Judea. They are seen to have a great measure of success. Following their empowering by the Holy Spirit, they have a dramatic impact upon their fellow Jews in Jerusalem.

It is quite clear from the context of Acts chapter 2 that the crowd which gathered together to hear Peter's first great sermon were Jewish men and women who had gathered together to celebrate the Jewish festival of Pentecost in Jerusalem. The fact that they heard the apostles speaking in the native languages of all the areas where they came from was a supernatural sign that God was doing something very special among them.

These Galilean Jews could not possibly have known all these different languages of the areas from which they were gathered. These Jewish people would have known both Hebrew, the language of their scriptures, and Greek, the language of trade and commerce. The Romans had kept Greek as the language of trade and commerce when they had taken over the former Greek Empire. Peter ascribed the sign of the apostles speaking in languages they had never learned as being a fulfilment of the prophecy of Joel chapter 2. The crowd would have recognised this as a prophecy of what would have taken place after the arrival of the Messiah.

Peter did not fail to point out the fact that some among their number had been among the crowd which had demanded the death of Jesus, their true Messiah. (See Acts 2:22-24). These verses cannot be taken as proof that his fellow Jews were alone to blame for Jesus' crucifixion. The rest of the New Testament clearly reveals that Jesus chose to lay down his life to redeem all mankind from the power and consequences of sin. (See John 10:17-18, 1 Peter 2:21-25, Romans 3:23 and Romans 6:23). It is clear from these verses that all people of all races are sinners and that Jesus voluntarily laid down his life for all of us. Therefore, we are all to blame for the crucifixion of Jesus. I will return again to this theme later in my book. What is beyond all doubt is that Peter's sermon had a tremendous effect upon those who heard him. Many of these people were brought to genuine repentance. Acts 2:41 suggests that at least three thousand people were added to the number of Jesus' followers as a result of this sermon. Furthermore, Acts 2:47 implies that every single day new people were added to the early church from among the Jewish residents of Jerusalem and Judea.

It soon becomes apparent from reading Acts chapter 3 that the apostles continued to attend the Temple in Jerusalem at times when prayer was offered. The healing of the lame man who had been lame from birth opened the way for Peter and John to proclaim to their fellow Jews, gathered at Solomon's Porch, their message regarding Jesus being the promised Messiah of Israel and saviour of all mankind. This action leads the early followers of Jesus into their first conflict with the official religious leaders of Judaism. The rest of the Book of Acts reveals continual opposition arising from these religious leaders against the Jewish followers of Jesus.

There is no doubt that these religious leaders feared the growing influence and popularity of Jesus' followers. It is also clear that the official religious leaders felt their positions of authority were threatened by this. From a casual reading of the Book of Acts, it is possible to reach the conclusion that the Jews were constantly opposing the followers of Jesus. However, this is a wrong conclusion. It was, admittedly, a large proportion of the Jewish religious leaders that opposed Jesus' Jewish followers. Yet, despite this fact, in Acts 6:7 Luke states that a great number of the Jewish priests became obedient to the faith, meaning clearly that they had put their faith in Jesus. This is a remarkable statement.

Putting their faith in Jesus would have had tremendous implications for them as individuals. They would have had to sacrifice all the wealth that working in the priesthood had brought to them. They would have had to resign from their positions on the Sanhedrin (the religious council of the Jews). Belonging to this council brought with it great honour and prestige. They would inevitably have had to learn new trades in order to support themselves and their families. Theologically they were the ones who held the most radically different beliefs from those of the early followers of Jesus. The priests belonged to the party of the Sadducees. They only accepted as scripture the first five books of the Bible, which the Jewish people call the *Torah*. They rejected any beliefs in life beyond the grave. They also believed that wealth was an indication that someone was living a life pleasing to God.

Jesus clearly confronted their beliefs in Luke 20:27-38. Here Jesus quoted the words of God to Moses in which he said that he would be forever known as the God of Abraham, Isaac and Jacob. (See Exodus 3:15). Jesus stated that this indicated that God was the God of the living and not the dead and that these men were forever alive in God's presence. Jesus' words caused even some of the scribes (Jewish rabbis who taught in the synagogues) to praise him for his wise answer that contradicted the Sadducees' beliefs. This was a very rare event indeed. The scribes, along with the other Jewish religious leaders, were more used to criticising Jesus' teaching and practices. One cannot overstate the importance of this insight of Luke regarding this particular group of the religious leaders being received into the company of Jesus' followers. It would have come as a tremendous shock to the religious leaders to see many of their number defecting into the ranks of the early church. It does, to some extent, explain why a wave of persecution would soon begin against the Jewish followers of Jesus. The religious leaders began to fear for their positions of power and wealth the more they witnessed numbers of even prominent members of their community putting their faith in Jesus.

From my analysis so far it is clear that the early church was remarkably successful in recruiting their fellow Jews into becoming disciples of Jesus. This vast increase in the number of Jesus' followers was to wonderfully prepare the way for the gospel to be proclaimed first to the Samaritans then to most of the Gentiles of the Roman Empire. It must also be remembered that the persecution of Jesus' followers that would soon arise was an entirely Jewish affair. It was the fearful, jealous religious leaders that launched a wave of persecution against the Jewish followers of Jesus. It was certainly not a case of the Jews uniting together to stop the teaching of Jesus from reaching the Gentiles. This wrong belief, held among some Christians, that the Jews were united against Jesus and all that he represented, is a very wrong one. To some extent this has been based on a wrong interpretation of John 1:11-12.

Some Christians have believed that when John wrote that Jesus came to his own and they failed to receive him that he was suggesting that most Jews failed to receive him. This is obviously a wrong interpretation of what John wrote. The rest of his gospel is packed with examples of Jews coming in great crowds to listen to Jesus. In his gospel even two of the top Jewish religious leaders identified themselves as Jesus' followers in paying for and organising his burial. Obviously John in these verses is referring to the sad fact that many of the religious leaders failed to recognise God's appointed Messiah which he had sent to them. They should have been the ones who were best prepared to receive and acknowledge him due to their in-depth study of the Jewish scriptures (what we Christians call the Old Testament). They should have been the first to recognise how Jesus so completely fulfilled the scripture's prophecies regarding the Messiah who would be sent first to Israel and then to the whole world. Many of the first to receive Jesus were ordinary Jewish men and women. It is also John who records Jesus' words, "Salvation is of the Jews." (See John 4:22).

The first episode of the conflict between Jesus' followers and the Jewish religious leaders is recorded by Luke in Acts 4:13-21. On this occasion the apostles were simply threatened that further preaching about Jesus would get them into trouble with the religious leaders. The leaders even chose to release Peter after he made it very clear that he had no intention of stopping his preaching regarding Jesus. It was probably due to the growing number of Jesus' Jewish followers that the religious leaders were reluctant to deal harshly with them. They feared that serious action against the leaders of Jesus' followers might lead to rioting. Riots in Jerusalem were the very last thing that they wanted. Any rioting would lead to them being called to account over it by Pilate, the Roman Governor of Judea. Pilate could, in extreme circumstances, strip the religious leaders of their power and authority. The Sanhedrin was only permitted to govern over Jewish religious affairs if it helped to keep the peace among Rome's Jewish subjects.

Even though the apostles continued their preaching after these threats had been made, the religious leaders were still reluctant to take decisive action against them. At the end of Acts chapter 5 Luke records the first beating that the apostles received as punishment for defying the religious leaders. It is interesting to note that even on this occasion Rabbi Gamaliel, a very senior leader in the Sanhedrin, actually intervened to stop serious action being taken against Jesus' Jewish followers. He is recorded as saying that if the Christian movement was only the work of men then it would eventually fizzle out; however, if it was really of God they could not stop it; in the end they might even find themselves fighting against God himself. It is only at the end of Acts chapter 7 that Luke records the first martyrdom of the first follower of Jesus at the hands of Jewish religious leaders who were opposed to the teaching of Jesus. It is at this stage that Saul of Tarsus first appears in Luke's record of the history of the early church. He is introduced as a senior Jewish religious leader who gives his approval to what the crowd is doing in killing Stephen. (See Acts 8:1). From this point onward, for a short while, Saul leads the Jewish religious leaders in an attempt to wipe out Jesus' followers by means of seriously persecuting them.

Saul's attempt to stop the spread of Jesus' teaching through persecuting his followers had entirely the opposite effect to that which he intended. By attempting to imprison Jesus' followers many of them left Jerusalem only to spread their message concerning Jesus to their fellow Jews beyond Judea to the other provinces of the Roman Empire. It is interesting to note at this point that the Jews were already represented in all the major trading centres throughout the Roman Empire. These scattered Jewish communities were then used by God as a springboard from which the gospel would be launched to the Gentiles.

The wave of persecution Saul launched against the followers of Jesus had another major effect in regard to the successful evangelism of Samaria. To state that a difficult relationship existed between Jews and Samaritans would indeed be a great understatement. The Samaritans were the products of inter-marriage between the Jews left behind from the Babylonian exile and Gentiles, mainly of Arab origin. They claimed that they worshipped the God of Israel and that the returning exiles had wrongly forbidden them to be involved in the worship of God at the Temple in Jerusalem. They believed that when the Messiah came he would end this division and rebuke the Jews for this action against them. A great degree of bitterness had grown up between the Jews and the Samaritans by the time Jesus began his public ministry. Most devout Jews would have rather taken a long detour across the River Jordan if they were travelling between the two Jewish provinces of Judea and Galilee. Jesus deliberately chose to go through Samaria and was even the guest of the Samaritans in a village of Samaria.

The account found in John chapter 4 shows just how far Jesus departed from the practices of the Jewish rabbis of his day. Even the woman at the well was completely shocked to find him asking for a drink of water from her, a Samaritan woman. She was even more shocked when later into the conversation Jesus declared himself to be the Messiah that both Jews and Samaritans were awaiting.

It is even more surprising to find John reporting that many of the Samaritans came to accept him as their Messiah through this visit. The religious leaders would have been greatly shocked to find Jesus making the Samaritan the hero in his famous 'Parable of the Good Samaritan' in Luke 10:30-37. On one occasion John reports the religious leaders insulting Jesus by saying that he was a Samaritan and had a demon within him. (See John 8:48).

In the light of these facts it is not too surprising to find Philip starting a very successful campaign of evangelism among the Samaritans in Acts chapter 8. The apostles quickly gave their backing to what Philip had begun by Peter and John being sent to preach alongside him and to pray for the Samaritans to receive the 'gifts of the Holy Spirit'. This action guaranteed that the followers of Jesus would never be accepted as just another sect within Judaism. They had by this action gone way beyond what most of the Jewish leaders could ever accept as being morally correct for Jews to do. This gulf between the Jewish religious leaders and Jesus' followers would widen even further when in Acts chapter 10 Gentiles were received as part of the Christian community without the requirements of having their males circumcised or obeying the ritual aspects of the Law of Moses. Yet despite what has been stated here, the Christian community still kept on growing among the Jewish people throughout the Book of Acts.

The conversion of Saul of Tarsus is an event of tremendous significance in the life of the early followers of Jesus and, indeed, has done much to shape the direction that Christianity would take for centuries to come. Saul was the leading figure in initiating the first great wave of persecution of the followers of Jesus. His conversion to the faith of the very community he tried so hard to destroy left the Jewish religious leaders in disarray. Luke reports that for a considerable time his conversion brought a return of peace to Jesus' followers. (See Acts 9:31).

In many ways Saul was the most unlikely vessel for God to use in his plan to share the gospel among the Gentiles. He came from a strict religious background as a Pharisee. Prior to his conversion, proclaiming the teachings of Jesus to the Gentiles he worked amongst would have seemed completely ridiculous to him. At the very least one could have expected him to have been the champion among Jesus' Jewish followers of those who wanted Gentile converts to follow the Law of Moses most strictly and for male converts to be circumcised. He had, after all, been brought up into the strictest form of Judaism found among his people. As we shall see, the reverse was actually the case. He became known as 'the apostle to the Gentiles'. In his letter to the Galatians, in chapter 2, Saul of Tarsus (who now became known as Apostle Paul) explained how he opposed those who wanted Gentiles to be circumcised and live strictly by the Law of Moses. He also explained to them how Peter and the other leaders of the followers of Jesus fully accepted that he was called especially to the Gentiles, to proclaim God's truth to them.

In Acts 15:22-35 Luke clearly sets out the decision of the leaders of the Christian community to accept the Gentile believers in Jesus as equals in the Body of Christ. In this passage Luke also makes it clear that the Gentiles are not required to be circumcised and to live strictly according to the ritual and ceremonial Law of Moses. However, it is also clear from these passages that there were a group of Jewish followers of Jesus who strongly held to the opposite view. They became known as the Judaizers. These men wanted the Gentile believers to be circumcised and live under the same rules as the Jews. The major theme of Paul's Letter to the Galatians is that these believers were trying to distort the gospel which Jesus had proclaimed and that Jesus' Gentile followers should actively oppose and reject the distorted views of these men.

Doctor Ron Moseley, in his article 'Evidence of the Jewish background of the early Church' notes the fact that the word 'Christian' was a late addition to the vocabulary of Jesus' followers. His followers referred to themselves as 'Followers of the Way'. Jesus' followers were most often identified as a sect within Judaism, not as a separate religion, during the years of the first century. There is no doubt whatsoever that many of Jesus' Jewish followers still attended the Temple until after its destruction in AD 70. Paul and other Jewish followers of Jesus found themselves regularly invited to speak in the local synagogues as they sought to tell their fellow Jews about Jesus, the Messiah of Israel.

Dr. Ron Moseley suggests, "The word 'Christian' does not come from the Hebrew word for the 'Anointed One' but from a Greek word, and it was not used by the Jerusalem Church at all. 'Christian' was first used as a Gentile title for the believers at Antioch some forty to forty-five years into the first century (Acts 11:26). There is no evidence that the term was used extensively as a self-designation by the early Church since it is only used three times in the New Testament and only once by a believer (Acts 11:26, 26:28 and 1 Peter 4:16)." I believe that comparatively few church members today are aware of this interesting fact.

Although it is very apparent from the New Testament that Paul was called to be the apostle to the Gentiles, it is equally clear that on all his missionary journeys he visited the Jewish synagogues on a regular basis and enjoyed a good measure of success in persuading his fellow Jews to follow the one he believed to be their one true Messiah: Jesus of Nazareth. (See Acts 14:1, Acts 17:1-4, Acts 17:10-12, Acts 18:1-4 and Acts 28:16-24). Although it is very clear from the Book of Acts that Paul faced opposition from jealous, unbelieving Jews, it is also most apparent that many of his fellow Jews came to faith in Jesus through him. Many of his fellow countrymen and women worked hard with him to help him succeed in proclaiming the truth he had found in Jesus to as many people as possible throughout the then known world. He and the other Jewish followers of Jesus risked their lives to proclaim the gospel to us as Gentiles. Some of them, including Paul himself, had to lay down their lives in order to achieve this goal.

Jim Gerresh suggests:

The Church in Jerusalem remained a Jewish Church for several generations. The historian Eusebius reports that the first fifteen bishops of Jerusalem, until the time of HHadrian (AD 135), were all Hebrews. After the fifteenth bishop, Narcissus, we finally hear of Marcus, who is listed by Eusebius as the first Gentile bishop of Jerusalem. He reports that the whole church consisted of Hebrews.[3]

I believe that if most Christians were aware of the facts they would show a great deal more appreciation towards the Jewish people. Knowing these truths should surely inspire us as Gentile Christians to oppose anti-Jewishness in all its forms and pray for Jesus' natural brethren to find their wholeness in knowing him as their Messiah. We should be inspired by these facts to oppose Replacement Theology as a false teaching - that it is totally inconsistent with both the Jewish origins of Jesus himself and the Jewishness of the early Church. It is most clear from this analysis of the early Church that at no time would any of Jesus' followers have called themselves Palestinians. The suggestion that this was the case, by some of the advocates of Replacement Theology, is totally ridiculous.

---

[3] *How did a nice Jewish Church become Gentile?*, Jim Gerresh

Jesus' Conflict with the Jewish Religious Leaders

Already in my first two chapters I have made some reference to the conflict which arose between Jesus and the Jewish religious leaders. It is without doubt one of the major themes running through all the four Gospels, and indeed the Book of Acts. In no way would I wish to minimise the importance of this theme. No one could develop a full understanding of the life of Jesus and his ministry without taking into account this important topic. In the same way, no one could develop a full understanding of how Jesus' apostles spread his message throughout the Roman Empire without considering how some of the Jewish religious leaders opposed their message.

However, the way this theme has been represented throughout Christian history has led many ordinary Christian believers to conclude that most Jews actively opposed Jesus and his message. It has led many Gentile Christians to blame the Jews as a race for the crucifixion of Jesus. This impression, backed by the misrepresentation of many of the Church Fathers in regard to this issue, has been to a great extent responsible for the persecution of the Jews by those who have claimed to be the followers of Jesus. As we shall see in this chapter, the translators of the New Testament have, on occasions, helped to reinforce this wrong impression.

We will at this point examine in greater depth why Jesus was opposed by many of the religious leaders of his day. One of the reasons for this opposition was undoubtedly the fact that Jesus had not spent the years of training in a rabbinical school like all the rabbis of his day had done. Jesus was undoubtedly trained as a carpenter not a rabbi. (See Mark 6:1-3). This led some of the religious leaders to question him as to the source of his authority to speak out on matters of religious importance. In Luke, chapter 20:1-8, we read of one occasion when both the Sadducees and the scribes (the rabbis) came together to ask Jesus by what authority he was teaching in the Temple and who had given him that authority. They would have claimed to have received their authority due to their training in preparation for their ministry. It was clear to them that Jesus lacked the official training to claim to have authority on the same grounds.

Jesus' question regarding the authority of John the Baptist to teach the crowds and baptise people left them in a terrible dilemma. He, like Jesus, lacked the official training to qualify him (in their opinion) to fulfil his ministry. Yet John the Baptist was widely regarded by ordinary Jews as being a great prophet. They did not want to say that John had no authority from God to fulfil his ministry. If they had said this they would have made themselves very unpopular among the ordinary Jewish people. If, on the other hand, they confessed that he had received this authority to fulfil his ministry from God, Jesus could have easily pointed out that John the Baptist had told the crowds that Jesus himself was the promised Messiah of Israel. Faced with this dilemma they refused to answer Jesus' question in regard to where John the Baptist had received his authority from. Jesus in return refused to answer their question in regard to the source of his own authority.

Jesus never opposed the moral code found in the Law of Moses. In Matthew's account of the Sermon on the Mount (Matthew 5, 6 and 7) Jesus quoted from various chapters of the Torah (the first five books of the Bible). Each time he confirmed the importance of what God had said through Moses. Each time Jesus went beyond the letter of the Law of Moses to interpret what was meant by it. What Jesus often opposed was the tradition of the elders. This tradition was basically rabbinical interpretation of what was written in the Torah. Mitchell Bard, in his article 'Pharisees, Sadducees and Essenes', explains the importance of the oral tradition to the Pharisees. It was, of cause, equally important to the scribes. He suggests:

> The *main distinguishing characteristic of the Pharisees was their belief in
> an Oral Law that God gave to Moses at Sinai along with the Torah.
> The Torah or Written Law was akin to the U.S. Constitution in the
> sense that it set down a series of laws that were open to interpretation. The
> Pharisees believed that God also gave Moses the knowledge of what these
> laws meant and how they should be applied. This oral tradition was*

codified and written down three centuries later in what was known as the Talmud.[4]

In Matthew chapter 15 Jesus was confronted by the accusation that his disciples were eating their food with hands that were unwashed. This had nothing to do with his disciples failing to follow the basic rules regarding personal hygiene. The accusation was that his disciples were failing to wash their hands in the way established by the tradition of the elders, the oral tradition. In his reply to this accusation Jesus sought to show how following this oral tradition strictly could lead to a man actually living in disobedience to one of the Ten Commandments. He quoted the commandment that everyone should honour their father and mother. Implicit within this commandment is the need to provide for our parents if they are in physical need due to adverse circumstances. Jesus went on to suggest that following the rule on giving to the Temple (called 'Corban') developed in the Tradition of the Elders, may lead to someone living in disobedience to God's commandment. Once a man had vowed to give a gift to the Temple, according to the Corban rule this gift had to be given within the agreed timeframe even if this money was needed to meet the needs of the man's parents which had arisen due to some unforeseen circumstances.

Jesus went on to say that this was one way in which man-made religious rules could rob God's word of its power. His description of the oral tradition was highly offensive to both the Pharisees and the scribes. They would have been very concerned that his words were undermining one of their central beliefs. They feared that Jesus' popularity amongst the ordinary Jewish people would cause them to disregard the oral tradition, thus undermining their credibility. The fact that the Sadducees also rejected the authority of the oral tradition did not threaten their credibility in the same way since the Sadducees had very little support among the ordinary Jewish people.

The way in which the tradition of the elders defined the things individuals were allowed to do or not do on the Sabbath Day led Jesus into other conflicts with the scribes and the Pharisees. One of the Ten

---

[4] *Pharisees, Sadducees and Essenes*, Mitchell Bard

Commandments stated very clearly that showing respect for the Sabbath Day was an important duty God expected the Jewish people to fulfil. Part of showing this respect for the Sabbath involved not doing unnecessary work on this day. The tradition of the elders defined which work was allowed by the commandment and which was not. For example all the religious leaders were agreed that you could give sufficient help to a sick man or woman on the Sabbath to prevent them from dying. However, you were not allowed to give sufficient help to them to make them well. One had to wait until the next day to offer this amount of help to the sick man or woman.

Similarly, a man was allowed to rescue a farm animal which had fallen into a ditch on the Sabbath. The tradition of the elders allowed this because the rabbis taught that God did not want animals to suffer unduly due to Jews obeying the Sabbath Law. It is astonishing that the tradition of the elders seems to rate avoiding animals suffering as more important than avoiding human beings suffering. Jesus pointed out this lack of credible consistency in the rules set up by the tradition of the elders in Luke 14:1-6. Having healed a man with badly swollen arms and legs, Jesus justified his actions by referring to the fact that the religious leaders allowed a farmer to save not only his son if he fell into a ditch on the Sabbath but even his ox. The question Jesus brought before them was, why should he not be allowed to relieve the suffering of this very poorly man on the Sabbath by bringing God's healing to him? Not one of the religious leaders offered Jesus an answer on this occasion.

I believe that they feared to answer this moral question that Jesus had brought before them because they did not want to be seen to contradict the rules set up by the tradition of the elders. There is no doubt that in every other way Jesus would have upheld the principle enshrined in this commandment that people should have one day each week as a day set aside for the worship of God and to rest upon. What Jesus opposed was the legalism of the scribes and Pharisees enshrined in the tradition of the elders. He completely rejected their belief in this oral tradition, believing that the Torah alone was inspired by God. It did not require an oral tradition to interpret it; thus God did not supply any oral tradition to Moses or to anyone else. Jesus clearly believed that this oral tradition was man-made. This legalism caused Jesus to conflict with these two groups continually each time that they witnessed him healing sick people on the Sabbath. (See Mark 3:1-6, Luke 13:10-17 and John 5:1-18). Jesus told the religious leaders in John 5:17 that the reason he did not stop the work of healing on the Sabbath was that God, his Father, never stopped from the work of healing on the Sabbath. This challenged the view of many rabbis that God himself stopped from all work on the Sabbath. I believe that Genesis 2:1-2 only suggests that God rested from his work of creating the universe on the seventh day (the Jewish Sabbath). I also believe that his work of healing mankind and sustaining his creation never ceases.

One account of Jesus' conflict with the religious leaders over the Sabbath rules they sought to establish and police reveals just how petty-minded some of these religious leaders had become. In Luke 6:1-5 Jesus was confronted by the Pharisees over the issue of his disciples partaking of grains of corn whilst walking through a field on the Sabbath. These Pharisees were not for one moment suggesting that they were stealing this grain. The Law of Moses instructed that the edge of farmers' fields were available for anyone who was hungry to eat from. Rather they were accusing them of working on the Sabbath. From the context of what was written in these verses, it seems that these religious leaders had nothing better to do than spend part of the Sabbath hiding out in the fields waiting to catch people engaging in such a minor indiscretion. These men considered rubbing a few grains together to be working. I believe that this story has a humorous element to it. I picture these men suddenly jumping out from the field where they were hiding, shouting with some level of self-righteous joy, "We've caught you doing what is not lawful on the Sabbath." This story could have a title written above it saying 'religious people do the funniest of things'. How deceived religious men and women can become when loving God and their neighbours ceases to be the aim of their lives. These Pharisees would no doubt have known in their minds the commandment to love God with every part of you and your neighbour as yourself. The sad thing is that this knowledge was only academic to them. It failed to influence the way that they lived from day to day.

Matthew chapter 23 is often seen as the section in the gospels where Jesus clearly exposes the hypocrisy of the scribes and Pharisees. However, this chapter begins by Jesus stating that much of what they taught from the Law of Moses was true and should be obeyed. (See Matthew 23:1-3). What Jesus criticised them for was their failure to live according to the underlying principle behind God's law that people should seek to love God with every part of them and their neighbour as they love themselves. They failed to let love be their guide as to how to live out the laws given to them by God through his servant Moses. This failure to let the principle of love become their guide, coupled with their pride, drove these religious leaders into the terrible spiritual blindness that hypocrisy leads to.

In this chapter Jesus expresses his great sorrow that these religious teachers have fallen into - the terrible trap of spiritual blindness through their pride and hypocrisy. I believe that we all need to take note of these things Jesus taught in regard to these religious leaders. Can we not all fall into spiritual blindness due to pride, hypocrisy and a lack of love towards our neighbour? In the light of these facts, it is clear that these are not anti-Jewish statements made by Jesus. Rather they are an expression of his sadness in regard to the deception of these religious leaders.

At the end of Matthew 23 Jesus expressed his sorrow over the failure of these religious leaders to recognise him as their true Messiah. He wept over their spiritual blindness. This blindness caused them to reject all God's attempts to draw them closer to him through the miracles they had seen Jesus perform and the wonderful teaching he had brought to them. Their spiritual blindness, Jesus foretold, would lead on to the destruction of the Temple in Jerusalem. Yet, despite all of this, in the last verse of this chapter Jesus foretold of a time when the Jewish people would once again see him and recognise him as their Messiah, the one who would come to them in the name of the Lord.

So far I have explained why many of the scribes and the Pharisees came into conflict with Jesus. Now I turn to examine why the other group of the religious leaders, the Sadducees, came to oppose Jesus. The scribes were the rabbis who looked after the scrolls on which the scriptures were written and taught the meaning of these scriptures in the synagogues. The Pharisees assisted them in running the synagogues. Both of these groups believed that the whole of the thirty nine books of these scriptures had been given by God to show the Jews the things that God required of them. The Sadducees, in contrast to them, were solely concerned with the running of the Temple in Jerusalem. The priests and their helpers, the Levites, belonged to this party. The Sadducees held beliefs that were very different to the scribes and the Pharisees. The Sadducees did not accept the thirty nine books of the Jewish Scriptures as inspired by God. They only accepted the Law of Moses, the Torah, as their scriptures (the first five books of the Bible). They rejected the oral tradition, believing that no other sources were required to help interpret the Torah. They also did not believe in life after death. We know less about this party than the Pharisees and the scribes, since no prominent figures belonging to their ranks wrote about their history and beliefs.

The 'New World Encyclopaedia' suggests:

Most of what we know about the Sadducees comes from their critics, including Josephus, who wrote that they were wealthy and powerful, and that he considered them boorish in social interactions.[5]

We also know that the Sadducees were not generally held in high esteem by the ordinary people. Their belief that there was no afterlife made their beliefs unattractive to many. The fact that they seemed very willing to collaborate with the occupying Roman authorities did not endear them to the ordinary Jewish people, who were highly resentful of Roman rule. The main reason that their opposition to the ministry of Jesus had such an important impact (and is often referred to in the Gospels) was that they held half of the seats on the Jewish religious council, called the Sanhedrin. Without their support in the Sanhedrin, the Pharisees were powerless in regard to fulfilling their plan to bring Jesus to trial before this council.

When Jesus challenged the beliefs of the Sadducees relating to there being no resurrection from the dead, his words were well received by the scribes. (See Luke 20:27-39). He even received words of praise from them. The scribes, and no doubt the Pharisees, would have been particularly

---

[5] *New World Encyclopaedia*

impressed by the way Jesus had quoted the words God spoke to Moses according to Exodus 3:15 to show that the Sadducees were wrong in their beliefs regarding life after death. God's words to Moses, that God would forever be known as the God of Abraham, Isaac and Jacob, were a definite indication that these patriarchs were forever alive in his presence. The Sadducees could not argue that Jesus was quoting scriptures which they did not accept. No one belonging to the party of the Sadducees would have been pleased with Jesus' open challenge to the validity of their beliefs.

Since the Sadducees were all involved in the administration of the Jewish Temple in Jerusalem and not the synagogues throughout the country, they only came into conflict with Jesus when he was in Jerusalem. No doubt they would have been made aware of Jesus' conflict with the scribes and Pharisees in the Sanhedrin, where representatives of all these groups met together to jointly govern the religious affairs of the Jewish people.

The first major conflict arose between Jesus and the Sadducees when Jesus cleared the traders out of the outer court of the Temple. These traders were given the right to trade in the outer court by the Sadducees in return for a large percentage of the profits that they made from their trading going into their pockets. Thus these traders were allowed to conduct their trading in the outer court of the Temple because the Sadducees profited so greatly from it.

According to the gospel writers, Jesus cleared the temple traders out of the outer court of the Temple on two separate occasions. John records Jesus clearing the traders out of the Temple right at the start of his ministry. Each of the writers of the Synoptic Gospels (Matthew, Mark and Luke) record Jesus doing the same thing at the end of his ministry, just a few days before his crucifixion. I don't think for one moment that John mixed up the chronology of his gospel account. No doubt John knew where the other writers had placed this incident since his gospel is widely acknowledged to have been the last to be written.

The Synoptic Gospels dwell at great length on the events of Jesus' Galilean ministry. John fills in the gap left by the other Gospel writers by informing us of some the events which took place in the southern province of Judea. John himself acknowledges the fact that all four Gospels combined could not contain everything that took place throughout the ministry of Jesus. (See John 21:25). At the start of Jesus' ministry John reports the fact that Jesus was challenged by "the Jews" regarding his right to expel the traders from the outer court of the Temple.

I believe the translators would have been far more accurate if they had indicated that these Jews were from the ranks of the Sadducees. (See John 2:18). I think the failure of the translators to indicate the fact that the Jews who opposed Jesus were from the ranks of the religious leaders arises from their false perception that it was "the Jews" as a whole race which opposed him. To me, this arises from the subtle influence of Replacement Theology. I will return to this theme later in my book. In any case, Jesus' refusal to perform a sign (miracle) to prove he had the authority given by God to act this way in the Temple would have annoyed the Sadducees intensely. To them, Jesus was an untrained man, behaving in an arrogant manner, which potentially threatened their authority to govern the Temple.

When Jesus entered the outer court of the Temple for a second time and again turned the traders out of this court, the Sadducees were in no doubt intensely angered by Jesus' actions. There is no doubt that Jesus' action in clearing the Temple was one of the major factors in causing the Sadducees in general to join a plot to have him executed by the Roman governor. The High Priest, Caiaphas, who co-ordinated this action of the religious leaders, was the leader of the Sadducees. The other main factor influencing the Sadducees to take a major role in the plot to have Jesus executed was the way the crowds welcomed him as their Messiah when he came riding on a donkey into Jerusalem. Although the Sadducees didn't believe that the writings of the prophets were part of their Scriptures, they were very aware that in entering Jerusalem on a donkey Jesus was making a claim to be the Jewish Messiah that the crowd were most aware of.

In Zechariah 9:9 the prophet had made the clear prediction that their king would arrive in Jerusalem riding on a donkey. The Sadducees, and many of the scribes and Pharisees, feared that exciting the crowds with claims that he was their Messiah might lead to violent disorder in Jerusalem. This disorder might bring the wrath of the Roman governor and his soldiers upon the whole of the Jewish people. If this were to happen it could lead to the religious leaders being stripped of their authority. They knew that the Romans only respected their authority in a land that they had colonised on the condition that the religious leaders would keep the Jewish people peaceful and compliant towards Roman rule. If the Roman governor came to believe that they had failed in this regard, they knew he would abolish their privileges and end their authority as rulers over the religious affairs of the Jews.

There is no doubt that their jealousy over Jesus' popularity among the ordinary Jewish people was a factor that caused many religious leaders to plot together to have him executed by the Romans. The fact that so many Jewish religious leaders came together to plot against Jesus seems, at least at first sight, to support the contention of the supporters of Replacement Theology that the religious leaders united together to get Jesus killed and that their action brought God's curse upon the Jews as a race. However, this is not the full story.

The high priest had to call a meeting of the Sanhedrin to conduct Jesus' trial at night and had to pay Judas a large sum in order to get Jesus betrayed at night. The reason for paying Judas to betray Jesus at night was that he was afraid to have Jesus arrested during daylight hours. He knew this could lead to the supporters of Jesus rioting. In a similar way, calling the Sanhedrin to meet at night is the action of a fearful man willing to break the rules normally followed by this committee. His reason for this is obvious. By calling a night-time meeting of the Sanhedrin he could exclude the scribes and Pharisees who supported Jesus from this meeting. He feared that if he called a regular, scheduled meeting of the Sanhedrin he might fail to get this body to condemn Jesus and to pass him on to Pilate, the governor, for sentencing. This certainly undermines the case of those who support Replacement Theology. They have to portray the Jewish people as being largely united against Jesus to justify their view that God justly condemned the whole Jewish race for rejecting him and supporting his crucifixion. This was certainly not the way things were historically.

One of the incidents quoted in support of their contention that God rightly rejected and punished the Jews for rejecting Jesus is the behaviour of the Jewish crowd at Pilate's Judgment Seat. They claim that this crowd represented the Jewish nation as a whole. They further claim that this crowd cursed their whole race when they said, "His blood be upon us and our children." (See Matthew 27:25). In response to this I would suggest that this crowd were totally unrepresentative of the Jewish nation. The fact that this crowd were gathered at Pilate's Judgment Seat early in the morning, following a feast night, is indicative that they were actually a rent-a-mob employed by the chief priest and his associates. The crowd appear to have waited on the religious leaders to follow their every cue. Even if this crowd had been representative of the Jewish nation, Jesus' prayer for his enemies would have brought to nothing their self-cursing. (See Luke 23:34).

It is surely most apparent that Jesus' conflict with the religious leaders arose out of Jesus' unique interpretation of the Law of Moses and the Jewish scriptures (which we Christians call the Old Testament). Jesus never questioned the validity or divine inspiration of these scriptures. Nor was he opposed by all the religious leaders. The opposition he faced from some of them did not reduce his popularity among most of the ordinary Jewish people. These factors certainly do not support the case of the supporters of Replacement Theology. They, in fact, seriously undermine their contention that the Jews, as a nation, were responsible for the rejection of their Messiah and for his crucifixion. It is evident that only a small minority of the Jews were responsible for doing these things. It is also very clear that on no occasion did Jesus ever blame all Jews for his rejection or crucifixion. The expression of his sadness at Jerusalem's rejection of his mission at the end of the twenty third chapter of Matthew's Gospel has to be read in the context of this chapter. Clearly Jesus laid the blame for his rejection firmly at the feet of the corrupt, hypocritical religious leaders. It was their spiritual blindness that led to the rejection of his mission.

Should Gentile Christians have to live like Jews?

This was an important issue that was discussed and resolved by the early church at the Jerusalem Council. Chapter 15 of the Book of Acts reports all the details of how this issue arose and was dealt with by the leaders of the early Church in Jerusalem. The issue arose because an increasing number of Gentiles (non-Jews) were coming to faith in Jesus and receiving baptism. Some of the Jewish Christians answered the key question "Should Gentile believers in Jesus have to live like Jews?" with the definite answer "Yes, they should!" Other Jewish Christians, led by Apostle Paul, were equally definite in their answer to this question. Their answer was "No, of course Gentiles should not need to embrace all the laws of Judaism in order to become members of the early Christian Church."

The Jews who demanded all Gentiles wishing to become members of the Church to be circumcised and become obedient to the Law of Moses became known as 'Judaizers'. These men were very vocal in their views. When they came into contact with Gentile Christians they argued that these Christians had not properly been received into the Church. They taught that the male Gentiles had to submit to the rite of circumcision and become converts to the Jewish Faith if they really desired to follow Jesus. In the act of circumcision these Gentiles would be expected to obey the Law of Moses - both its moral law and its ritual law. The decision of the Apostles at the Jerusalem Council was a major setback to this group but did not completely end their activities.

One of the main purposes of Apostle Paul's letter to the Galatians was to warn them against the influence of the Judaizers which had disturbed the faith of this largely Gentile Church. In Galatians 5:1-9 Paul warned these Gentile believers not to undergo the physical act of circumcision and pledge their allegiance to follow the Law of Moses in all its details. He told them that if they submitted themselves to this wrong teaching then they would enter into something that God had not intended for them. Paul also explained how having faith in Jesus led all his true followers to undergo a spiritual circumcision of their hearts done by the Holy Spirit working within them.

The requirements that the early Church leaders wanted the Gentile Christians to fulfil are given in Acts 15:23-29. They were required to avoid food which had been offered to idols, from the meat of strangled animals, from eating blood and from deliberate sexual sin. By fulfilling these requirements the Gentile Christians enabled Jewish Christians to feel comfortable fellowshipping with them. Had the Church leaders in Jerusalem demanded Gentile converts to be circumcised and endeavour to obey every detail of the Law of Moses, it is most unlikely that Christianity would have spread so successfully among the Gentiles and that Christianity would be the largest world religion today. This was a very brave decision by the leaders of the early Church, who were at this time predominantly, if not entirely, Jewish. In making this decision they effectively separated Christianity from Judaism. A minority of Jewish Christians refused to obey this ruling and actively opposed it. This party of Judaizers was constantly in conflict with the apostle Paul.

Over the years Christian leaders who emphasise the importance of recognising the debt of love we as Christians owe to the Jewish people have been wrongly labelled as Judaizers. It has been a slow process for the congregation which I lead to fully accept the Jewish origins of our faith in Jesus. We are now fully united in regard to the issue of celebrating the Jewishness of Jesus and reaching out to his natural brethren with love and understanding. We now enjoy celebrating God's feasts along with the Jewish people. We see in them aspects which looked forward to the coming of Jesus as the Messiah of Israel. This has been brought about by God's grace working among us and through faithful teaching over the years regarding this vital issue.

Inevitably a small minority of our congregation have moved to find their spiritual homes in other church fellowships over the years. Over the years we have had some very amusing incidents occurring due to the failure of some of our congregation to understand the Jewishness of Jesus and the debt that we owe to the Jewish people as Christians.

One of the most comical happened when one of our older ladies reacted very badly to a new lady arriving at our Sunday evening service.

The new lady came and greeted me with the lovely greeting, "Shalom, Pastor Frank."

('Shalom' is the Hebrew word of greeting, which translated means 'Peace be with you'. It was the word Jesus used to greet his disciples after his resurrection). I greeted her in a similar manner. She then went around the fellowship greeting other people with the same greeting. All was going well until she greeted this certain elderly lady.

She responded with the words, "Don't shalom me; I don't want shalom-ing."

Our visitor tried to explain, in vain, how the greeting she had used was a beautiful greeting used by the risen Jesus when he had met his disciples immediately after his resurrection.

The old lady answered, "I hate Jews. They killed Jesus. Our pastor is trying to turn us all into Jews."

My heart sank in sorrow. Where had this old lady been, in her mind, when I had so often taught the scriptures revealing how wrong her views were? Years of being taught by church leaders who had been influenced by Replacement Theology had twisted her mind to oppose the truth whenever it was taught. The old lady left our fellowship for a while but then returned a more humble woman. Thankfully, she repented of her anti-Jewish views and apologised to me regarding them before the Lord called her home. God answered our prayer for her in a wonderful way.

It is interesting to note that the leaders of the early Church came far short of demanding that Gentile Christians be required to keep all Jewish food laws. Jesus taught that all foods were clean according to Mark 7:14-23. Apostle Paul, in a similar way, taught that all food is made clean by the prayer of thanksgiving (see 1 Timothy 4:1-5). This does not mean that Jews who are fulfilled in knowing Jesus as their Messiah have to give up living by a 'kosher' diet. The apostle Paul made it clear that all Christians should respect one another as regards their choice of diet in his letter to the Church at Rome (see Romans 14:1-17). This clearly means that a church fellowship should be prepared to keep to the kosher food rules if Jewish people request that this should be the case. However, it equally means that Jewish members of a church fellowship have no right to demand that other members of the fellowship should live by kosher diets in their own homes. Similarly, Jewish believers in Jesus can still seek to have their children circumcised due to the fact that this rite is an important part of Jewish culture. The fact that the apostle Paul encouraged Timothy, whose mother was Jewish by race, to be circumcised can be quoted in support of my view relating to this issue (see Acts 16:1-3). Paul knew that Timothy needed to embrace his Jewishness if he were to become acceptable to his fellow Jews.

Unfortunately some Gentile Christians who stand up for the Jewish people and acknowledge the great debt we owe to them as a nation go to extreme lengths in order to identify with them. This involves wearing Jewish clothes for worship, putting a 'mezuzah' on the doorpost (a mezuzah is a box which contains quotes from the Torah) and getting circumcised without there being any medical reason to do this. This kind of behaviour is actually offensive to Jews. They really do not want Gentile Christians to do this. Some Gentiles attempt to teach other Gentiles that they must adopt Jewish food rules in order to become acceptable to God. All these actions go against the ruling given by the Church leaders at the Jerusalem Council, reported to us in Acts chapter 15.

Christian Zionists would always seek to correct the wrong views of extremists who go beyond the decisions of the Jerusalem Council. We are obviously supportive of the Messianic movement, both within the borders of Israel and throughout the nations. We believe that the restoration of the State of Israel in 1948 was the fulfilment of biblical prophecy. We also believe that the survival of the modern State of Israel is a miracle of God's grace. I am always keen to quote Malachi 3:6 in support of my beliefs regarding this issue. This verse clearly suggests that the fact the 'sons of Jacob' are not consumed is due to God's unchanging nature. The 'sons of Jacob' referred to in this verse obviously means the Jews as a distinct national grouping. All Christian Zionists join together in seeking to oppose the doctrine of Replacement Theology. Sadly the actions of this tiny minority of extremist Zionists tend, to some extent, to undermine the effectiveness of our efforts. I personally gladly embrace the label of 'Christian Zionist' or 'Zionist Christian'. However, I am keen to stress the fact that I do not support the beliefs of the Judaizers which Apostle Paul did so much to contend against in his letters to the various churches. I am also keen to defend the fact that we as a church fellowship celebrate the biblical feasts that God gave to the Jewish people. These feasts, along with the Feast of Dedication (Hanukkah), were celebrated by Jesus and his disciples. I believe that participating in these feasts helps us to understand more about Jesus himself. I strongly believe that the later Church Councils were wrong to attempt to stop church members from celebrating these feasts.

Later in this book I will attempt to explain how the poisonous doctrine of Replacement Theology influenced the decisions of all the Church Councils which have occurred since the biblical Church Council which met at Jerusalem.

Going back to the question that I posed at the start of this chapter, it is clear to the reader that I certainly don't believe that Gentiles should try to live like Jews. I support fully the rules laid down by the Jerusalem Council. I sincerely believe that a different answer to this question is actually biblically wrong and reveals a lack of understanding in regard to what will help more Jews to receive Jesus as their Messiah. I need to make my theological position clear so that I can teach the truth in love to my fellow believers in Jesus regarding the issue of Replacement Theology. I will under no circumstance defend behaviour which I consider to be unbiblical and even counterproductive to the cause of undoing the negative influence of Replacement Theology upon the body of Christ.

Finally, let me refer to a rather comical conversation I had with a fellow believer. Brother P, who would describe himself as a Messianic Christian, had a real problem over the food other Gentiles eat. He and his wife ran a thoroughly kosher kitchen. On one occasion he suggested to me that no church fellowship in the entire area he lives in is sound enough for both him and his wife to attend. He went on to say that the church fellowship which I lead is at least on the right lines in many ways. However, he went on to suggest that they could only join our church fellowship if I could give him an assurance that my other church members and I would permanently give up eating pork and pork products in our homes. He wanted us to sign a pledge that we would adhere to this policy. When I attempted to explain why I could not commit either the church fellowship or myself to conform to his rules he suggested that they would continue to enjoy ministering to the Lord on their own.

I said in response, "I am sure that the Lord must really look forward to your ministry. I wonder how he managed to survive without your ministry before you were converted."

I don't think Brother P appreciated my sense of humour.

The Origin of Replacement Theology in the Church at Rome

The Church in Rome, no doubt, had its origin arising from the Jewish community which traded in the city and settled in the city. The apostle Paul wrote his letter to this church to set out his theology. In a sense, this letter is unique among his letters. The other letters to the Christian churches in the major cities of the Roman Empire arose out of their pastoral needs. In particular Paul wanted to correct problems which had arisen within these churches either as a result of false teaching influencing the church members or due to the church members failing to let the Holy Spirit transform them into the image of Jesus, their Lord and Saviour. When Paul wrote to the church in Rome he was writing to a community he longed to visit but had, in fact, had no influence in establishing.

However, this is not the whole story in regard to Paul's letter to this church. There was at least one pastoral issue that Paul wanted to address. This was the issue of disunity within the church arising because of an underlying conflict between the Jewish members of the Church and some of its Gentile members. These Gentile members had fallen into the sin of pride. As I mentioned previously, the issue of a large proportion of Jews failing to recognise Jesus as their Messiah was a theological problem facing the entire body of believers in the early Church. Indeed, if we are honest, this issue has perplexed Christians over the centuries of Church history. Natural human logic suggests that if the Jewish nation had been prepared by their Scriptures to recognise their Messiah then his arrival should have been overwhelmingly recognised and welcomed by this nation. Sadly, this had not occurred when Jesus came as the Messiah of Israel.

The apostle John expresses his sorrow relating to this issue right at the start of his gospel, in his prologue.

John wrote, "He came to his own and his own did not receive him" (see John 1:11).

One can detect a degree of frustration in the mind of John as he wrote these words. Paul clearly felt the same sadness and frustration as John when he was writing to the church at Rome. In Romans chapter 9

Paul expressed his pain and sorrow in regard to the failure of so many of his fellow Jews to recognise their true Messiah, Jesus. In verse 3 of this chapter Paul even stated that he would have been willing to have been cut off from Jesus if by this action the rest of his natural brethren, the Jews, would have then accepted and obeyed him. The rest of chapters 9, 10 and 11 of his letter to the Romans contains Paul's attempt to explain why so many Jews failed to recognise Jesus as their Messiah.

Replacement Theology is one attempt at explaining why so many Jews failed to recognise their Messiah. From reading Paul's letter to the church at Rome it is clear that at least a significant number of Gentile members had embraced the doctrine for this very reason. Advocates of Replacement Theology suggest that the reason why so many Jews rejected Jesus as their Messiah is that they were inherently stubborn, lacking in faith, and hypocritical as a race. They portray Old Testament history as the Jews' failure to show themselves deserving of God's election and choice of them as the chosen people. They conclude that the inherent sinfulness of the Jews has caused God to reject them as the chosen people and to replace them by the Gentile Church as his new chosen people. Some of those who teach Replacement Theology refer to the Gentile Church as 'the new Israel'. All those who teach this doctrine agree that God's reason for rejecting the nation of Israel and choosing Gentiles instead is that the Gentile Church would bear much better fruit in his service than Israel had produced. Teachers of Replacement Theology seem unaware of their own arrogance in making such conclusions about God and his choice of those whom he would call to serve him.

In Chapter 11 of Romans, Paul sought to rebuke the Gentiles in the church at Rome who had reached the conclusion that God had chosen them to replace the Jews in his plans. In verses 19 to 21 Paul addressed these proud Gentile Christians and warned them to get rid of their pride by repenting of it. They were told not to boast about themselves over the Jews whom God had removed like natural olive branches from their tree. They, as Gentiles, had been grafted in as "wild olive branches" simply because of their faith in Jesus. They had not earned this privilege. If they became proud and started to be boastful in regard to the Jewish people,

Paul warned them that God could choose to remove them from the olive tree.

Paul's analysis of God's relationship to the Jewish people in chapters 9, 10 and 11 of his letter to the Romans reveals the fact that God is most certainly not a 'replacement God'. This, as we shall observe, undermines the whole argument of those who attempt to teach the doctrine of Replacement Theology. In verse 4 of Romans chapter 9 Paul states the fact that it was through the Jews that the worship of the true God was revealed to the world. In the next verse Paul points out to all Christians that it was through the Jews that Jesus was born into the world. Thus, in fact, God's choice of Israel did fulfil his purpose in choosing them. In the rest of this chapter Paul makes it clear that throughout the history of his dealings with the Jewish people God has always worked through a faithful remnant of them to fulfil his purposes. In Romans 11:28 Paul states a most remarkable truth. He states that because of the faithfulness of the patriarchs (Abraham, Isaac and Jacob) he will always bless the Jews as his chosen people. He will always accept them as his friends.

Paul then goes on to state the fact that God never changes his mind over whom he chooses and whom he blesses. It is due to these facts that Paul makes the remarkable prophecy that a whole generation of Israel will turn to God and put their faith in Jesus as their Messiah. This very event was also prophesied by the prophet Zechariah in the Old Testament (see Zechariah 12:10-14). I don't think any respected Bible scholar has ever suggested that these verses have as yet been fulfilled in Jewish history. I fail to see how these verses can be applied in any way to the Church. I believe with all my heart that this last great spiritual revival is yet to occur. In support of my view I would also cite the prophecy of the prophet Ezekiel given in Ezekiel 37. In this chapter Ezekiel not only speaks of God restoring the people of Israel back to their own land from the 'land of the north' (meaning their restoration from the Babylonian exile) but also of God bringing them back to their own land from all the nations where they have been scattered (see Ezekiel 37:21).

I believe that this can only refer to the Jews being gathered to their own land in the 20th and 21st centuries following the restoration of the State of Israel in 1948. Ezekiel then makes one more remarkable prophecy. Following this physical restoration (bringing the Jews back physically to their own land) Ezekiel suggests that the Jews will be wonderfully restored spiritually to serve God. Ezekiel suggests that this will occur when "a king like David will be their king" (see Ezekiel 37:21-28). This supports the accuracy of Apostle Paul's prophecy regarding the whole of Israel being saved and bringing God's blessing to all the nations. In the light of these prophecies it is surely most clear that Replacement Theology is based on the unbiblical belief that God has once and for all rejected the Jews. Rather than seeking to replace the Jewish people and rob them of their wonderful role in bringing God's spiritual blessings to the whole world, surely the whole Church should be praying for the wonderful fulfilment of these prophetic scriptures. The entire Church should be rejoicing at the thought that God has planned to bring such spiritual riches to the ends of the earth.

I believe passionately that Replacement Theology is in fact the opposite to the teaching of Apostle Paul in his letter to the Romans. I also believe those who advocate this doctrine misrepresent the nature of God. They fail completely to recognise the fact that God will once again bless all the nations when the Jews embrace their true Messiah, Jesus. Thankfully, God is unchanging in his nature and is not a 'replacement God'.

In conclusion, it is clear that Paul ruled out Replacement Theology as a valid explanation of why many Jews had been blinded from accepting Jesus as their Messiah. He tried to root out this wrong belief from among the Gentile Christians in the church at Rome. I find it absolutely astounding that the Church Fathers failed to recognise this fact when so many of them went off in the direction of Replacement Theology. I find it even more astounding that Martin Luther, the great Protestant reformer, failed to take note of Paul's teaching regarding the issue of Replacement Theology.

The Book of Romans was quoted by Martin Luther more than any other book of the Bible in his writings. Sadly, Martin Luther became one of the leading advocates of the doctrine of Replacement Theology. Chuck Cohen, in his book 'Roots of Our Faith', points out the negative impact he believes has taken place within much of the Church as a consequence of so many Christians failing to understand and respect the Jewish roots of their faith in Jesus. He suggests:

Much of the Church has acted, and still acts, as though it has been grafted into a Christmas tree- flashing its attractive lights and decorations, but it is unconcerned about its loss of roots and wondering why it is spiritually drying up and dying.

I fully agree with his conclusion regarding much of the Church. It is my great desire that through reading the pages of this book, and taking on board the issues it raises, many of my fellow believers in Jesus will come to experience a renewal of their spiritual life as they come to love and respect the Jewish people, through whom God has brought to us all the riches of the gospel. I believe that when we come to acknowledge the Jewishness of Jesus we begin to understand him much better. We enjoy wonderful spiritual blessings when we pray for his blessings to come upon his people. At no point does our love for the Jewish people cause us to hate the Arabs. Rather we pray for them to find in Jesus real abundant life and weep over the way that militant Islam has blinded so many of them and set them upon a path of violence and self-destruction.

The Role of the Church Fathers in Defining and Promoting Replacement Theology

The Church Fathers undoubtedly did much to define and explain Christian beliefs. Many of these men lived saintly lives. However, in regard to the relationship of Christians to the Jewish people they have had an appalling long term impact. Their words have been ianquoted in order to justify the most terrible atrocities that have ever been committed against any ethnic group in human history. These atrocities have been committed against the natural brethren of Jesus himself, the Jewish people. On occasions these atrocities have even been committed in the name of Jesus. There is little wonder that many of the Jewish people are intensely suspicious of the motives of Christians when the gospel is presented to them.

The Church Fathers actually defined and established the doctrine of Replacement Theology. The Church Councils set up regulations governing the relations between Christians and Jews that would completely divorce Christianity from its Jewish roots. These regulations were justified according to the writings of the Church Fathers.

Before examining the words of the Church Fathers relating to the issue, it is important to examine the historical factors which influenced their thinking in regard to the relationship of Christianity to the Jewish people.

The Romans did not try to impose their religion or language on the nations they conquered. They maintained Greek as the language of trade across their empire because much of it was taken from the Greek empire that preceded the Roman empire. In the same way, the Roman emperors believed the best way to guarantee the stability of their empire was to work with the religious leaders in the nations they had conquered, on the condition that they agreed to work with the Roman governors to keep the peace in their countries.

For the Jews this meant that they had complete autonomy regarding their religious affairs; this meant that they were even allowed to have their own currency to operate within their temple. The Romans allowed the Jews to enforce their own laws regarding their religious affairs. The

Sanhedrin (the Jewish religious council) could even impose fines and beatings on their fellow Jews as punishments if they failed to adhere to their religious laws. This meant that most of the Jewish religious leaders were fairly supportive of Roman rule. As regards the ordinary Jewish people the situation was entirely different. Most of them resented Roman rule. Some went much further and formed the Zealots, a band of fighters which conducted guerrilla warfare against the Romans.

Before AD 70 there was a reluctant acceptance of Judaism by the Roman authorities. It was due to Roman acceptance of Judaism that the first Jewish followers of Jesus sought to represent themselves as a sect of Judaism. This began to change due to the Jewish revolt against Roman rule in AD 70. As a consequence of this revolt and the destruction of the Temple in Jerusalem, a wave of anti-Jewishness swept across the empire. The Jews were forced to leave Jerusalem and were scattered across the empire. From then on Jews were regarded with a degree of suspicion by the Roman authorities. Romans came to believe that all Jews were disloyal to the Roman Empire. They believed that they owed a higher level of loyalty to the Law of Moses than to the state. Many Romans believed that the Jewish practice of circumcision was barbaric and should be banned across their empire.

In 132 AD Emperor Hadrian tried to forcefully ban this practice across the Roman Empire. By this time the number of Gentiles belonging to the Church outnumbered the Jewish believers. The leaders of the Church consequently became predominantly Gentile. These leaders feared that this outbreak of persecution against the Jews would lead to a fresh outbreak of persecution against the Church. It became increasingly expedient for these Church leaders to stress the separation of Christianity from Judaism, even if this action was offensive to the Jewish Christians. Clarence Wagner in his article 'The Error of Replacement Theology' writes:

> *Many Gentile Christians interpreted the destruction of the Temple as a sign that God had abandoned Judaism, and that he had provided the Gentiles freedom to develop their own Christian theology in a setting free from Jerusalem's influence ... After the second Jewish Revolt (AD 133-135) put down by the Roman Emperor Hadrian, theological and*

*political power moved from the Jewish Christian leaders to centres of
Gentile Christian leadership such as Alexandria, Rome and Antioch. It
is important to understand this change because it influenced the early
Church Fathers to make anti-Jewish statements as Christianity began to
disconnect itself from its Jewish roots.*

Many Gentile preachers started to actively blame the Jews for
rejecting Jesus. Obviously this stopped the advance of the message of
Jesus among the Jewish people. Increasingly, the Jewish people began to
perceive Christianity as anti-Jewish.

The very first of the anti-Jewish statements of the Church Fathers
was written by Marcion in 160 AD. He decided that he needed to purge
the Church of what he perceived as dangerous Jewish errors and
influences. It is interesting to note that he reached this conclusion at the
very time a fresh wave of persecution was being launched against Jews
across the Roman Empire. No doubt Marcion thought that this attempt to
distance Christianity from Judaism would help to shield Christians from
persecution. Irenaeus felt inspired to speak out against the Jews in
180 AD. He explicitly blamed them for the death of Jesus and suggested
that God had punished all Jews for this act of wickedness. Only by
forsaking their Jewishness, he suggested, could individual Jews be forgiven
for their ancestors' wickedness.

Hippolytus (170-236 AD) was another of the early Church Fathers
to state openly that all the Jews deserved to suffer for rejecting Jesus as
their Messiah. He suggested that Christians should not in any way attempt
to stop this happening or they would find themselves in opposition to the
will of God. Eusebius of Caesarea was the next Church Father to make
anti-Jewish statements. He stated that God would most certainly punish
the Jewish race for rejecting Jesus. He claimed that God's punishment
would mean that the Jews would never again be allowed to rebuild
Jerusalem (quote taken from 'Zionism and Israel Encyclopaedic
Dictionary'). His prediction has been clearly shown to be completely
wrong due to the fact that the Jews have returned to Jerusalem and have
rebuilt the city. They were able to take full control of Jerusalem in 1967
after victory in the Arab-Israeli war. As a result of the statements of these
Church leaders several Church Councils made anti-Jewish rulings between

341 AD and 620 AD. These Church Councils prohibited Christians from "celebrating the Jewish Sabbath, celebrating Jewish festivals and even eating a meal with an unconverted Jew"[6] .

Church members were threatened with the penalty of excommunication if they broke the restrictions that had been imposed upon them. As a consequence of these Church Councils, Jews who wanted to identify themselves as Christians had to deny all aspects of their Jewish culture. It is interesting to note that according to the rulings of these councils Jesus and his disciples would have faced excommunication (expulsion) from the very Church that they had established if they had continued doing the things they did during Jesus' public ministry. No one had the courage to challenge the illogical nature of the rulings of these Church Councils.

I am most happy to inform you that I have broken every one of these Church Council rulings. I often worship Jesus at public meetings on both the Jewish Sabbath (Saturday) and Sundays. I regularly celebrate each of the feasts that God gave to Israel. I have often led the celebration of these feasts in a similar way to the way my Saviour would have led them. I have also had the privilege of having a meal with non-Messianic Jews on several occasions. One of these Jews even put their faith in Jesus as their Messiah after I had several discussions with them over food. I sincerely hope that I would have had the courage to speak out against the rulings of these apostate Church Councils had I been alive during their times.

One of the most outspoken Church Fathers who promoted Replacement Theology was John Chrysostom. He was a highly respected theologian, whose name meant 'golden mouthed'. However, when it came to the Jewish people he made some of the vilest, racist statements ever made against an ethnic group. Michael Brown, in his book 'Our Hands Are Stained with Blood', quoted the words of Chrysostom:

The synagogue is worse than a brothel ... it is the den of scoundrels and the repair of wild beasts, the temple of demons devoted to idolatrous cults... the refuge of brigands and debauchees and the cavern of demons. It is a criminal assembly of Jews... a place of meeting for the assassins of

---

[6] *Christian Hatred and Persecution of the Jews,* Phyllis Petty

*Christ... a house worse than a drinking shop... a den of thieves; a house of
ill fame, a dwelling of iniquity, the refuge of devils, a gulf and abyss of
perdition.*

Michael Brown commented on these words. He wrote:

*What happened to Christian love? He had wished that he had been
cursed in place of his Jewish people. Chrysostom instead cursed them.
How much destruction was subsequently ignited by these tragic sermons of
malice?*

I find it almost beyond belief that learned men like Chrysostom
could fail to see how their words were so much in opposition to the words
of Jesus himself who taught his followers to "love your enemies and do
good to those who hate you." They also failed to take seriously the
implications of Jesus' words "No one takes my life from me, but I lay it
down and take it up again." (John 10:18) I find it almost unbelievable that
Chrysostom could actually write that the Jews were Christ's assassins if he
had ever read these words of Jesus. It is sad to think that so many
Christians throughout Church history have failed to realise that it was the
sin of each one of us that took Jesus to the cross. In the light of this fact,
how can anyone blame the Jewish people for the death of Jesus? If the
Jewish people cannot be blamed for the death of Jesus then there is no
way anyone can suggest that they were rejected and cursed by God for
killing him.

Some leaders of the Church opposed Christians who actively
persecuted the Jews, yet they still held to the belief that the Jews were
rejected by God for rejecting and killing Jesus. Pope Innocent III tried to
stop Christians actually persecuting the Jews but at the same time
represented the Jews as cursed of God and condemned to wander the
earth for the crime of killing Jesus. He wrote:

*The Jews against whom the blood of Jesus cries out ought not to be killed,
lest the Christian forget the divine Law.*

Sadly he went on to write:

...as wanderers they should roam the earth until their faces be filled with shame.

Pope Innocent wanted Christians to punish Jews for killing Jesus by "trade boycott, social ostracism, expulsion from all offices of authority and trust." If he was considered a protector of the Jews whilst still holding this terrible attitude towards them, does not this reveal how appallingly the poison of the Church Fathers' attitude towards the Jews had affected other Christians?

St. Augustine of Hippo (AD 354-430) took up this same theme in his sermon against the Jews. Clarence Wagner writes:

Augustine asserted that even though the Jews deserved the most severe punishment for having put Jesus to death, they had been kept alive by divine providence to serve, together with their scriptures, as witnesses to the truth of Christianity. Their existence was further justified by the service they rendered to the Christian truth, in attesting through their humiliation, the triumph of the Church over the synagogue. They were to be a 'witness people'- slaves and servants who should be humbled.

Augustine also popularised the allegorising of biblical passages as a valid method of understanding the true meaning of the Bible. He asserted that the Bible was full of hidden meanings which could only be understood by deep reflection. He suggested that the promises given to Israel in the Old Testament should no longer be interpreted literally. They should be interpreted spiritually and applied to the Church. He was adamant in his belief that God had finished dealing with the Jews as a chosen people. Their role as instruments through which God would reveal his purposes to mankind had ended with the birth of the Church. Their rejection of Jesus had sealed their national fate. Only by embracing the teachings of the Church could individual Jews be set free from the curse that their ancestors had brought upon them.

Augustine taught covenantal theology. He taught that God could only have one body of people to represent him in the world, not two. In

the Old Testament the body that represented him was the nation of Israel.
Since the death and resurrection of Jesus, the Church alone represented
God. In this sense the teachings of Augustine are the basis of covenantal
theology, the cornerstone upon which the beliefs of all those who
advocate Replacement Theology are based.

It is important to note that Augustine's method of allegorising
biblical texts is not based upon any explicit biblical teaching. Rather this
method of interpreting biblical passages arose from the influence of Plato,
the great Greek philosopher. Thus Platonic philosophy, of non-biblical
origin, through Augustine has had a major theological impact upon
modern Christian theologians as to how they seek to interpret the Bible.
Due to the great regard with which the writings of Augustine are held by
Roman Catholic scholars, Lutheran scholars and Calvinist scholars, the
poisonous doctrine of Replacement Theology is still influencing thousands
upon thousands of church ministers today. The influence that the writings
of Augustine had upon them was openly acknowledged by both Martin
Luther and John Calvin in their writings. He shares the blame with these
reformers for the negative impact of Replacement Theology upon the
Jewish people down the centuries. The fact that Martin Luther became a
major proponent is relatively well known. His vicious anti-Jewishness will
be analysed in some detail in this book, due to the fact that his writings
were the great inspiration that encouraged Adolf Hitler to plan the mass
murder of the Jewish race, which we now refer to as 'the Holocaust'.

However, the fact that John Calvin advocated Replacement
Theology is not so well known. Dr. Paul Wilkinson, in his article
'"Prophets who Prophesy Lies in my Name": Christian Palestinianism and
the Anti-Israel Crusade', asserts:

> John Calvin (Jean Cauvin) was the most influential of the sixteenth-
> century Reformers. Like Martin Luther, he was Augustinian in his basic
> theology and eschatology. He was also a covenantalist, or advocate of
> 'covenant theology', teaching that there has only ever been one people of
> God 'the Church' and one covenant of God 'the covenant of grace'.
> Calvinism teaches that the Church has replaced, or superseded, Israel.

Calvinist teachings are also an inspiration to the advocates of Replacement Theology as much as the writings of Martin Luther. Both reformers imbibed the poison of Replacement Theology through Augustine and the other Church Fathers. Both of these reformers rejected the concept of a literal one thousand year reign of Christ upon this earth through his influence. In rejecting belief in a literal millennial reign of Jesus, they also rejected the idea of a literal rapture occurring and any belief in God bringing a wonderful national revival among the Jewish people. They rejected any idea of the Jewish people being ever restored again to the land of Israel. The prophetic promises regarding any future blessings of God coming upon the Jewish people were totally discredited by both of these reformers. These promises were spiritualised and applied to the Church. There is, therefore, little wonder that so many Protestant theologians have adopted these beliefs and encouraged other Christians to embrace them.

The dreadful suffering of the Jewish people by those who professed to be the followers of Jesus can be blamed largely on the anti-Jewishness of the Church Fathers. It must be noted that this anti-Jewishness arose directly from the doctrine of Replacement Theology. The laity (the majority of church members) was not inherently anti-Jewish. Rather it was the Church leaders who stirred up this animosity. Clarence Wagner states:

> *During this early period, the virulent Judeo-phobia was primarily limited to the clergy, who were always trying to keep their flocks away from the Jews. However, later, the rank and file, and the growing middle class would be the main source of anti-Semitic activity.*

Before closing this chapter regarding the impact of the Church Fathers in regard to forwarding the doctrine of Replacement Theology, it is important to consider some of the atrocities which occurred to the Jewish people in direct response to their words. The reason I have so often quoted the words of Michael Brown is due to the fact that his book has played such an important role in inspiring me to write this one. It is fitting, therefore that I should quote his words relating to this issue.

During the long dark years of the Middle Ages, Jews were given the option of baptism or expulsion, baptism or torture, baptism or death. Every type of degrading law was passed against them. They were forbidden to hold good jobs; after all, they were an accursed people, assassins of Christ, so how could they be allowed to prosper? They were forced to listen to humiliating public sermons aimed at their conversion- wasn't this the holy obligation of the Church? Their children were kidnapped and baptised as 'Christians', thus saving them from the fires of hell. They were rounded up and beaten as a highlight of Easter celebrations, since they deserved it all as murderers of the Lord.

Undoubtedly, on many occasions beating of Jews went much further, and they were murdered by mobs inspired by the hatred of their clergy.

Life for Jews who were willing to convert to Christianity was not easy. They were certainly not welcomed with open arms. They were always viewed by Church leaders with a degree of suspicion. Michael Brown suggests:

There was a witch hunt against baptised Jews who maintained any vestige of Jewishness. These Catholic Jews (called 'Marranos' or 'New Christians'), violently forced to convert in the first place, were carefully watched to see if they were practising 'heresy'. Heretical practices included failure to eat pork; failure to work on a Saturday; failure to wear their best clothes on a Sunday; keeping the biblical feasts; observing any Jewish customs of any kind; saying any Jewish prayers; preparing food according to Jewish law; associating with non-baptised Jews; and intermarriage of children of Marrano families with children of other Marrano families.

It is very clear that Jews who were converted to Christianity were expected to renounce all aspects of their Jewishness. Jews in Protestant countries were not treated any better. In these countries Jews who converted were regarded with an equal degree of suspicion. They too were expected to renounce all aspects of their Jewishness if they were to achieve any degree of acceptance by their fellow Gentile Christians.

There is no doubt in my mind that had it not been for the appalling anti-Jewishness of the Church Fathers, Martin Luther would probably never have condemned the Jews with the violent language he used regarding them. He was undoubtedly inspired by their rhetoric. He was undoubtedly influenced by their reasoning, justifying all forms of active discrimination against the Jews. Had it not been for the impact of Martin Luther, Adolph Hitler would have found it that much harder to recruit ordinary Germans to the cause of the violent destruction of the Jewish people. In this way one can observe a direct link between the anti-Jewishness of the Church Fathers and the events of the Holocaust. All this arose from the poisonous influence of Replacement Theology.

This doctrine has created a legacy of pain among the Jewish people which is still evident today. In my opinion, only genuine love and understanding can bring a healing from this pain. Christians need to sincerely apologise to the Jews for what has taken place wrongly in the name of Christianity. All believers in Jesus need to be informed of the Jewish roots of our faith in him. They need to be taught regarding the debt we all owe to their ancestors for bringing the message of the gospel to us as Gentiles. Without faithful Jewish Christians sharing the gospel with the Gentiles at the risk of their lives, and for some the cost of their lives, there would be no Christianity today.

Martin Luther and his Condemnation of the Jewish People

No one can doubt the bravery of Martin Luther in launching his campaign to bring an end to the dreadful corruption of the Church of his generation. As he read the words of the Bible he became aware of how far the Church had fallen from the standard God had set. His courage led him to be the first Church leader in the States of Germany to speak out against these abuses. All Christians in the Protestant tradition owe to him an acknowledgment of his bravery and a degree of respect for what he achieved during his lifetime. However, this should not blind reformed theologians from being highly critical of his hateful words towards the Jewish people. No one who studies the words of Luther regarding the Jews in his book 'The Jews and their Lies' can doubt the link between his vicious words and the cruel persecution of the Jews that culminated in the Holocaust.

Jim Walker, in his article 'Martin Luther's dirty little book: On the Jews and their lies' points out that Martin Luther played a major role in promoting anti-Jewishness among Christians. He suggests:

> *Although Luther did not invent anti-Jewishness, he promoted it to a level never seen before in Europe. Luther bore the influence of his upbringing and from anti-Jewish theologians such as Lyra, Burgensis and John Chrysostom. But Luther's book... took Jewish hatred to a new level when he proposed to set fire to their synagogues and schools, to take away their homes, forbade them to pray or teach, or even to utter God's name. Luther wanted German society to be rid of them and requested that his government and ministers deal with them.*

Luther even went so far as to suggest that Christians would not be at fault in God's sight for killing Jews since the Jews were guilty of killing Jesus. At this point Luther did not even suggest that Jews which had converted to Christianity should be exempt from this process. At this stage in his life he had reached the conclusion that Jews were not even worth converting. There is no doubt that had Luther gained the support of the German princes he would have launched an even greater campaign of violence against the Jewish people. The princes that supported Luther were preoccupied to a great extent defending their territories from the attacks of the Catholic rulers which were attempting to stop the growth of Protestantism.

In his early years Luther held a fairly positive attitude towards the Jewish people. He believed that the Jewish community across Europe had been prevented from embracing Jesus as their Messiah by the appalling corruption and idolatry that they had observed in the Church. He suggested that once the Church had been purged of these terrible abuses they would convert in large numbers to the reformed version of Christianity which he had established. In his book 'Jesus Christ was a Jew' Luther wrote:[7]

> *Perhaps I will attract some of the Jews to the Christian faith. For our foolish popes, bishops, sophists and monks have been coarse blockheads. If I had been a Jew and had seen such idiots and blockheads ruling and teaching the Christian religion, I would rather have been a sow than a Christian. For they have dealt with the Jews as if they were dogs and not human beings.*

Luther wrote this in 1523, early in his ministry, shortly after his actions had started the Reformation and he and his followers had broken away from the Roman Catholic Church. Luther, right from the very beginning, had little understanding of Jewish culture. He never sought to explore the Jewish origins of the Christian faith. Thus he never sought to establish his reformed version of Christianity in such a way that it was attractive to the Jewish people. He never sought to understand the feasts that God had given to Israel and the importance of the Sabbath to the Jewish people. Like the Catholic Church leaders he so eagerly condemned them as fools and blockheads; he sought to get the Jewish people to abandon all aspects of their Jewishness if they would be admitted into the fellowship of his newly-established form of Christianity.

---

[7] Source: Jim Walker's article

The success of the worldwide Messianic movement is testament to the fact that when Jesus (Yeshua) is presented in a sympathetic manner and Jewish culture is celebrated, not repressed, many Jews are willing to embrace him as their Messiah. Increasingly, many predominantly Gentile fellowships are celebrating God's feasts given to Israel and are enjoying celebrating the Jewish heritage of Jesus. The fellowship I lead has Messianic Jews within it but is predominately Gentile in its membership. Yet we thoroughly enjoy celebrating God's feasts. We do this, knowing that we have been grafted into the olive tree (representing God's blessing to mankind through Israel). All our members rejoice to know that we are blessed alongside the Jews - not in replacement of them. We feel blessed to know that one day a whole generation of the nation of Israel will be fulfilled in their Messiah, Jesus. Paul prophesied that when this occurs it will bring life from the dead to the whole of mankind (Romans 11:25-32).

Sadly, Luther failed to recognise these wonderful truths found in Paul's letter to the Romans, despite the fact that much of the inspiration that led him to start the Reformation came from this letter. Had not Luther been predisposed to turn against the Jews by the influence of Replacement Theology found in the writings of the Church Fathers, the Reformation might have had a wonderful impact upon the Jews of Europe. The fierce rhetoric of Luther would then have never been turned upon the Jewish community.

Martin Luther turned against the Jews in the latter stage of his life when he was subject to bouts of ill-health. The trigger for his outburst against the Jews was some blasphemous comments regarding Jesus being written by some Jews. There is no doubt that his anger boiled over after a long period of growing anger against the Jewish community. The reason for this growing level of anger on the part of Luther was most certainly due to the Jews appearing largely unmoved by the new Protestant version of Christianity. Luther's pride was wounded when the Jews failed to fulfil his expectation that most of them would quickly be converted and become part of the Protestant community across the German States. He then raged against them in a manner that even surpassed the worst anti-Jewish writings of the Church Fathers.

Is there Death in the Pot?

It is beyond any doubt that the writings of Luther were a major inspiration in the life of Adolph Hitler and his anti-Jewishness. Hitler himself acknowledged this fact. In 1924, eleven years before he came to power in Germany, Hitler addressed a Christian conference. He said to his mainly Lutheran audience:[8]

> *I believe today that I am acting in accordance with the will of Almighty God. I announce to you the most important work that Christians should undertake is that of getting rid of the Jews once and for all... Martin Luther has been the greatest encouragement of my life ... He was a giant. He saw that the Jews need to be destroyed and we're only beginning to see that we must finish his work.*

The most shocking thing was that on this occasion no one showed any dissent in regard to what Hitler had said. Martin Luther had helped to create an atmosphere in Germany in which it was acceptable to speak out against the Jews. Both the Protestant and Catholic leaders failed to raise any vocal opposition to his racist policies until long after he had achieved political power in Germany.

Michael Brown states in his book 'Our Hands are Stained with Blood' that both Catholic and Protestant Christianity are to blame for making the Holocaust possible. He writes,

> *Christianity did not create the Holocaust; indeed Nazism was anti-Christian, but it made it possible. Without Christian anti-Jewishness, the Holocaust would have been inconceivable. Hitler and the Nazis found in medieval Catholic anti-Jewish legislation a model for their own, and they read and reprinted Martin Luther's virulently anti-Semitic writings. It is instructive that that the Holocaust was unleashed by the only major country in Europe having approximately equal numbers of Catholics and Protestants. Both traditions were saturated with Jew-hatred.*

It should be noted at this point that the blame for Christians hating the Jews can be attributed entirely to the doctrine of Replacement Theology. Jesus' famous words "By their fruit you will know them" need

---

[8] *Christian Hatred and Persecution of the Jews,* Phyllis Petty

to be applied in this context. If the appalling fruit of the Holocaust can be attributed directly to the doctrine of Replacement Theology then surely this is further evidence that this doctrine is in itself morally wrong. It is right to conclude that the words of Luther regarding the Jewish people reveal the fact that he failed to understand the true meaning of his master's teaching in regard to Christian love and forgiveness. Had he understood this teaching he would never have gone into a rage when some Jews wrote blasphemous words regarding Jesus. Had Luther understood something of the debt that we Christian Gentiles owe to Jesus' first Jewish followers he would never have written such wicked words regarding their kinsmen.

Although most Christian denominations have now made statements rejecting the extreme anti-Jewishness of some of the Christian leaders, the beliefs of Replacement Theology continue to influence the thinking of many Christian leaders today. The churches have not condemned Replacement Theology as unbiblical and unchristian. The direct link between the theology of the Church Fathers and Martin Luther and the events of the Holocaust is not acknowledged by some Christian writers. Many Protestant writers seem reluctant to pay much attention to the issue of Luther's anti-Jewish attitudes.

Only by acknowledging this dreadful history can Christians begin to understand the mindset of the Jewish community today. This has to be the starting point for genuine dialogue to take place between Jews and Christians. A major section of the Christian Church is still perceived as anti-Jewish by many Jews. This problem is compounded by the fact that many Christians openly side with the Arabs in the Arab-Israeli conflict. They deny the Jews the right of self-defence and condemn the Israeli army for defending their land from terrorist aggression. I am not in any way defending human rights violations on either side. However, such Christians fail to recognise the constant corruption and human rights violations which occur in the Palestinian territories. They fail to understand the extent of the great division among the Palestinian leaders. The Palestinian group called Hamas, which governs Gaza, has consistently refused to recognise the right of the State of Israel to exist. The feud between Hamas and the other Palestinian group, Fatah, has been only papered over. These factors make it extremely difficult for Israel to negotiate any meaningful and secure peace with the Palestinians.

The biased attitude of some Christian leaders was shown by their decision to commend a boycott of Israelis among their church members. Such Christian leaders have been rather mute in regard to the repressive behaviour of the many Arab dictators in regard to their own Arab citizens. It seems that they are only willing to speak out when the Israeli armed forces appear to be acting aggressively. I suggest that this inconsistent behaviour arises from the subtle influence of the doctrine of Replacement Theology upon these church leaders. Whilst few Christian leaders would support all the anti-Jewish statements of Luther and the Church Fathers, their influence is still apparent in regard to their thinking. This influence is installed through the training most ministerial candidates receive in the U.K. in their theological seminaries and colleges.

The Sad Fruit of Replacement Theology

No one has established an accurate number of Jewish people who have been killed by Christians down the centuries. Although the Holocaust was the worst expression of anti-Jewishness, the number of Jews who perished in this deliberate attempt at genocide is still only a fraction of the vast number murdered overall. Considering the fact that well over six million Jews perished in the Holocaust this is a very sobering thought.

After AD 70 the might of the Roman army was frequently turned upon the Jewish people. The Gentile leaders of the Church tried to keep Christians free of this persecution by deliberately emphasising the differences between Judaism and Christianity. The doctrine of Replacement Theology provided the concept that could justify this separation between the two. It also provided the justification for Christians failing to defend the Jews when they were persecuted for simply being Jews and holding fast to their culture and their way of life. If they were rejected by God and cursed for their role in rejecting and killing their Messiah then Christians could rejoice when the Roman government punished them. They could sit back and let the Jews be ill-treated because, after all, this ill-treatment arose because of their sin.

Up until the time of Emperor Constantine, Gentile Christians remained passive observers in regard to the sufferings of the Jews. This all changed after the professed conversion of Constantine to the Christian faith in AD 306. Christianity became the established religion of the empire in AD 312. Clarence Wagner, in his article 'The Error of Replacement Theology', wrote:

> *Overnight Christianity was given the power of the Imperial State, and began to translate the concepts and claims of the Christian theologians, against the Jews and Judaism, into practice. Instead of the Church taking this opportunity to spread its gospel message in love, it truly became the 'Church Triumphant', ready to vanquish its foes.*

As early as AD 313 Constantine issued the Edict of Milan granting favour to the Christian faith whilst banning the Jews from worshipping in their synagogues. Thus the Jews were forced to worship only in their homes or to meet together in secret for worship. In AD 315, encouraged by Christian leaders, Constantine issued a further edict banning Jews from holding high office in the Roman Empire and forbidding Jews from serving in the army. Jews were also forbidden from attempting to convert anyone to follow Judaism. Anyone breaking this rule faced execution. Jews started to be executed by the first 'Christian' Emperor for merely attempting to follow their religion and culture. He was actively encouraged to do so by Christian leaders. This was only the beginning of the 'triumphant Church' actively persecuting the Jews using the state to enforce its wishes.

Up until the start of the Crusades many Jews were executed by the Christian State for breaking anti-Jewish laws. On many occasions, Christian mobs, inspired by the clergy's anti-Jewish sermons, attacked Jewish families and murdered them. These mobs were rarely brought to justice for crimes against Jews. Christian rulers even sought payment from wealthy Jews to use the law for protection from violent mobs. If payment was not forthcoming then the law was not used and mobs were free to steal property and murder them without any fear of arrest or punishment. Jews were blamed for stealing Christian children and using their blood to make their unleavened bread, poisoning the wells so as to spread disease among Christians and even stealing communion bread (the Host) to desecrate it in blasphemous rites. The clergy openly encouraged their congregations to believe these myths to keep them opposed to the Jewish people whom they blamed for killing Christ. These myths often led to mobs murdering Jews. On other occasions Christian rulers confiscated Jewish property at will and expelled them from their kingdoms. Jews suffering from these expulsions were often condemned to die in poverty.

The Crusades signalled the systematic murder of thousands upon thousands of both Jews and Muslims. The popes urged kings to join in a holy war to take control of the holy sites for the sake of the Church. The promise of the forgiveness of all sins was used as an inducement to get kings to either join in the fight for the Holy Land themselves or to send the best of their knights to engage in the conflict on their behalf. Anyone dying in the conflict was promised eternal life in Heaven as all their sins would be forgiven automatically in return for their efforts in this conflict. Hence the ends automatically justified the means. Any amount of cruelty toward Muslims (which were labelled 'Saracens') was thus justifiable. Similarly, any amount of cruelty towards Jews was wholly justifiable. The parallel with the conduct of the extremist Muslims today and this dark period of Church history is an obvious one. Both the 'Christian' Crusaders and the extreme Muslim Jihadists have used the concept of fighting in a holy war to justify acts of barbarity perpetrated against innocent men, women and children.

During the reign of the Ottoman Sultans, Jews were treated with a degree of respect by these Muslim rulers. They were protected by the rule of law in Muslim-ruled Palestine. Jews were allowed to repopulate Jerusalem and rebuild sections of the city. This was entirely reversed during the brief period when the Crusaders took control of Palestine. When Jerusalem first fell into the hands of the Crusaders, Jews were massacred along with Muslims. Those murdered by the Crusader army included men, women and children. The Jews that gathered in their synagogue in Jerusalem were burnt to death by the Crusaders. As Jewish men, women and children burned to death in their synagogue the Crusaders sang a hymn of praise to Christ: "O Christ we adore thee." These men seemed totally unaware that they were murdering the natural brethren of Christ. Such is the spiritual blindness that Replacement Theology creates amongst Christians. Wherever the Crusader armies went in the Holy Land, Jewish men, women and children were humiliated, tortured and murdered at the hands of these soldiers. As these Crusader armies set off for their travel to the Holy Land from their own lands they often attacked, tortured and murdered any Jews that they came across on their journeys.

No accurate estimate of the number of Jews murdered during this sad time of Church history has been made. What can be said is that the Crusader soldiers believed that any sins of barbarity against Jews and Muslims were automatically forgiven by God. They were encouraged to think this by their popes, bishops and priests. Most of them were unable to read the Bible for themselves due to the fact that many of them were illiterate. Even if some of them could read words in their native language they could not read the Bibles in Latin that were found in the churches. Latin was the language of the Church and of kings and princes. It is certainly interesting to consider who God will hold as most guilty for these dreadful atrocities committed in the name of Christ when he judges the secrets of men's hearts. I believe that those most worthy of blame are the Church leaders whose words instigated these atrocities, including many of the Church Fathers who were the first clerics to inspire Christians to hate the Jews.

Having surveyed some of the terrible events of the Crusades it is easy to understand why the word 'crusade' is regarded with such loathing by both Jews and Muslims. Yet even now some insensitive Christians use this word to describe some of their outreach services. Many of these Christians are insensitive simply because they are unaware of the terrible history. It is hardly surprising to note the fact that many Jews find the symbol of the cross to be offensive to them. The cross was the symbol found displayed prominently on the uniforms of the Crusader soldiers.

The terrible events of the Crusades are still deeply embedded in the consciousness of both Muslims and Jews. When speaking of my faith in Jesus to people of these faiths I find myself having to apologise to them for these things were done in his name. Michael Brown, in his inspirational book 'Our Hands are Stained with Blood' points out the fact that Christians can only be effective in sharing about the love of Jesus with non-Messianic Jews when they have shed many tears of repentance over the sins committed in our name against the Jewish people. He rightly reiterates this point several times in his book. The burden of my heart is to inform my fellow Christians of how Replacement Theology has brought so much hurt and death to Jesus' own race so that they can share with me the sorrow I feel in regard to how Christians have treated the Jews down the centuries of Church history.

Following the dark historical times of the Crusades, Jews continued to suffer from outbreaks of intense persecution across the nations of both Western and Eastern Europe. In Britain, throughout the Middle Ages, Jews found themselves banned from professions, restricted as to where they were permitted to live and, at times, expelled from the country. They were blamed for causing disease among Christians by poisoning the wells, kidnapping and murdering Christian children and even stealing the bread used in the mass or communion in order to insult Christ (commit blasphemy against him). In terms of evidence used against them, there were always 'confessions' from Jews made after they had been tortured. Regardless of the nature of this evidence against the Jewish community, most Christians, including most of the clergy, actually believed that the Jews were to blame for these crimes. Little wonder then that mob violence would often break out against the Jews. What happened in Britain was repeated across continental Europe.

Of particular note were the actions of the Cossack armies against the Jews of Russia. They stand out because of the vast number of Jews murdered by these Eastern Orthodox Christians and the ruthless efficiency with which these Jews were murdered. Behind this dreadful persecution was sadly the support of the Russian Orthodox senior clergy. During the Nazi occupation of Soviet Russia many of the ordinary Russian citizens were only too willing to cooperate with their Nazi invaders to surrender Soviet Jews to be murdered by them. Some even joined the Nazi death squads to assist them in carrying out Hitler's Final Solution.

In the former Soviet Republics today anti-Jewish propaganda is freely circulated. Far right parties, which advocate forced expulsion of the Jewish people and open discrimination against them, are very popular. Jews are often mentally and physically abused in the streets and their homes and synagogues vandalised. In response to this, senior Orthodox clergy have remained largely silent. Some have even spoken out in favour of discrimination against the Jews.

During the Counter-reformation, throughout Catholic Europe, the Jews were the target for open persecution. The Inquisition, in the Catholic nation of Spain, stands out in regard to the cruelty of the systematic persecution launched against the Jews.

It is estimated that 30,000 Marranos (Spanish Jews) were burnt at the stake in Spanish Inquisitions from the fifteenth century until 1808. In addition to this, in 1492, all non-baptised Jews were expelled from the country. Stripped of all their possessions, and without any means to defend themselves, the sentence of mass expulsion against these poor souls was virtually a sentence of mass death. Those who converted did not fare much better. They were treated as second-class citizens by other Catholics and just one wrong move could consign them to the fire.⁹

Jews who were observed to waver in their Christian faith were cruelly treated and openly humiliated before they were granted forgiveness by the 'Mother Church'. This involved being led through the streets, bareheaded, barefooted and naked down to the waist. Catholic Christians crowded together to observe their humiliation with a perverted joy. Church leaders encouraged them to jeer at these fallen Jews.

After their humiliation they were signed once more with the sign of the cross with the words, "Receive the sign of the Cross which you denied and which, being deluded, you lost."

On many occasions false accusations by non-Jewish Catholics brought this punishment upon individual Catholic Jews and their families. The word of non-Jewish Catholics was always considered more trustworthy than the word of a Catholic Jew. Even after this ceremony at a Catholic cathedral the punishment of penitent Jews continued.

Rafael Sabatini, in his book 'The Spanish Inquisition', states:

After this dreadful ceremony penitent Jews were whipped in procession on each of the following six Fridays, being naked to the waist, bareheaded and barefooted; they were expected to fast on each of those Fridays. They were disqualified for the rest of their lives from holding office, benefice, or honourable employment. They were also forbidden from using gold, silver, precious stones, or fine fabrics.¹⁰

If these penitent Jews broke any of the restrictions they would be condemned for heresy and burnt at the stake. Their families were also subjected to the same punishment. Having surveyed these appalling ways in which Spanish Jews were treated, Michael Brown posed a couple of important rhetorical questions.

---

⁹ *Our Hands are stained with blood,* Michael Brown
¹⁰ *The Spanish Inquisition,* Rafael Sabatini

Whose side do you think God was on? Is it possible that he approved of the methods and dogmas of the apostate Church of that day?

I think these are important questions which need to be asked. My answer to these questions is that I believe that the true God was very much on the side of the oppressed Jewish people. I believe all Christians should feel a degree of shame in regard to these dreadful events which occurred in the name of Jesus. It is hard to believe that it took up until the 1960s for the Roman Catholic Church to officially repudiate the views of the Church Fathers which were so anti-Jewish.

On the other hand it must not be forgotten that the Protestant Church in Germany hosted Hitler in 1924 and applauded him when he promised to get rid of the Jews. As we have seen, all the major groupings of Christianity have been guilty of anti-Jewishness. The sad thing is that Christians in the late twentieth century could write appallingly anti-Jewish statements and still be received and applauded by other professing Christians.

The representative view can therefore advocate love for the Jew, while being able to reject his anti-Christian nation that persecutes Christians and butchers other people who need Christ as much as they do. It can work for the conversion of Israel without becoming a pawn of a maniacal nationalism, a racial supremacy as ugly and potentially oppressive as its twentieth century arch enemy, Aryanism[11].

Such words obviously flow from a man who seems completely unaware of the fact that it was professing Christians who persecuted Jews throughout Church history - not the other way around. The question arises as to which Christians the State of Israel has actively persecuted. Unlike many of the Arab nations in the region, Israel's constitution guarantees religious freedom and her free judiciary enforces this guarantee. To even suggest that Israel's actions of self-defence against Palestinian terrorism are comparable to the actions of Nazism in Europe is absolutely ridiculous. His words reveal that this fellow believer is completely out of

---

[11] *Does Israel have a Future?*, Ray Sutton

touch with what has taken place in the Middle East since the establishment of the State of Israel in 1948. He also seems out of touch with the reality of the horrendous events that arose out of the Aryan (Nazi) policies of Adolf Hitler. Undoubtedly this man has a distorted perspective on events due to the poisonous doctrine of Replacement Theology upon him. He has partaken of the poison in the pot.

Pike, another twentieth century Christian theologian, wrote:

...we have unearthed irrefutable evidence that Israel is a dominant and moving force behind the present and coming evils of our day. To our amazement we find that Israel is not that trusted, familiar friend we thought we had known. Rather she is a misshapen facsimile of everything we had so fondly bid farewell to... We are at last confronted with a monstrous system of evil which, if unresisted will destroy us and our children and bring the entire world into such darkness, oppression, and satanic dominion that only the coming of Jesus Christ can make right again.

What 'irrefutable evidence'? I would suggest that the main threat to world peace and freedom arises not from the State of Israel but from the forces of Islamic fundamentalism. Such is the fruit of Replacement Theology. Pike, in my opinion, is completely out of touch with what is happening both in the Middle East and the wider world. He is unable to discern what is really taking place in the world today.

It is hardly surprising that many Jews are sceptical concerning the Church's awareness of its persecution of the Jewish people over the centuries. The Jewish author, Meir Simcha Sokolovsky, wrote concerning the Jews' perception of Christian opposition to their race:

From his birth, every Christian, practicing or nominal, imbibes the belief that the Jews, any and every individual Jew, are answerable for the murder of his Messiah. Indeed, the overwhelming majority of the acts of persecution, religious coercion and massacres suffered in history by our people came at the hands of the Christians. Thus we see that Christianity was a significant and major cause of Jewish suffering.

Although I believe that this author has stated his case beyond that which facts would support, I sympathise greatly with his opinion. Undoubtedly, far too many Christians do believe that the Jews are to be blamed for the death of Jesus. Thankfully not all Christians believe this lie. A significant number of Christian ministers are determined to do all we can to combat it. Sadly, I cannot oppose Meir's contention that professing Christians have been to blame for most of the Jewish people's suffering throughout history. I believe that this statement is an accurate summary of how Jews have suffered so terribly at the hands of those who have professed to be the followers of Jesus.

Thankfully there are many Christian leaders throughout Church history who have spoken out in support of the Jewish people. As we shall observe in a later chapter, these leaders have sought to contradict the beliefs of those who have supported Replacement Theology. They have sought to expound biblical prophecy in relation to the glorious future for Israel that God has planned. These leaders can be collectively called Christian Zionists.

If you are ever wondering about the extent to which Replacement Theology has influenced Christians in the UK I would ask you to make enquiries regarding the theological position of our main Bible Colleges and Seminaries regarding Israel. In the end I decided to complete my Masters' Degree online with a Theological Seminary in the U.S.A. All the institutions I contacted in the UK proved unwilling to offer me a course in Church history which majored in the sad relationship between the Church and the Jewish people. One lady, in charge of admissions at a certain Bible College, was asked if her college had any policy regarding Israel and the Jewish people. She seemed completely stunned by my question. Her reply amazed me. She asked me why I thought that her college should have any policy regarding Jews as God himself had enacted their own curse upon them. She then asked me if I was a Jew. I quoted her Malachi 3:6, suggesting that God does not change and that this verse indicates that this fact is the main reason why the Jews are not consumed. Her response stunned me. She asked me where you could find this book in the Bible. She went on to confess the fact that she was a New Testament Christian and did not bother much with the Old Testament. She claimed that she was also amazed by the fact that I, as a Gentile minister of religion, should be so concerned about the Jews.

Combating the Arguments used by those who Promote and Defend the Doctrine of Replacement Theology

From the outset the importance needs to be stressed of someone having the right motivation and the right methods when seeking to help other believers to be set free of wrong doctrine. I remember on one occasion confronting some Jehovah's Witnesses on my doorstep as a newly qualified graduate. At university, Theology had been my main subject. I was determined to tear their arguments into shreds.

They soon became aware of my biblical knowledge. With my mum having a proud smile on her face regarding her son's intellectual prowess, I was really enjoying exposing their lack of ability in defending their beliefs. After they had made their excuses and left, I inwardly congratulated myself on a job well done. I simply did not realise how proud I was. The Holy Spirit soon revealed to me how wrong I was in my motivation when 'witnessing' to this Jehovah's Witness couple.

In my inner man I recognised his voice saying, "Yes you won the argument but failed completely in your mission to reveal the love of Jesus to that elderly couple."

I felt tearful and had to repent of my wrong attitudes toward those I was seeking to witness to.

My appeal to Christian believers who are aware of just how wrong the beliefs of Replacement Theology are is that we need to keep a humble, prayerful attitude towards other Christian believers who have been blinded by this wrong doctrine. We are called to "contend for the faith" (Jude v3). This involves explaining to other Christians how they might have been deceived by false teaching. The only way to do this is by going to the Bible to show them why some of their beliefs are not in agreement with what the Bible teaches. My aim in writing this chapter is to equip my fellow believers who already have a love for the Jews so they can present biblical truth to those deceived by Replacement Theology. However, at the same time I wish to offer a challenge to anyone who sincerely believes in Replacement Theology to review their arguments in the light of the

Scriptures I am quoting and make up their own mind as to whether or not their beliefs regarding the Jews are in agreement with the teachings of the Bible.

At the very centre of the arguments that most proponents of Replacement Theology use to put forward their view is their claim that God has rejected the Jewish people due to their role in the rejection and death of Jesus. Upon this premise the whole case for Replacement Theology is built. If this plank is demonstrated to be unbiblical then it becomes clear that the whole teaching is unbiblical.

At this point let me add that it is important to ask for the leading of the Holy Spirit before entering into debate with someone over the issue of Replacement Theology. The same thing needs to be said about all discussion of the truths which God has revealed in the Bible. Jesus himself made it very clear to his disciples that it is the role of the Holy Spirit to lead us into all truth (John 16:13). Ask God to clear the minds from any demonic deception of all involved in any important biblical discussion. We are warned most seriously of the danger of demonic deception (1 Timothy 4:1). It seems most terrible to me to know that people can be so deceived by evil spirits that they can depart from a true and genuine faith in Jesus and be led into error. I believe that Replacement Theology is one of the most powerful deceptions to arise and that the Prince of Darkness and his demon host are very involved in promoting it.

Proponents of Replacement Theology often give special attention to the Parable of the Tenants found in Matthew 21:33-46. This parable is different from most of Jesus' parables in that every part of it is an allegory. The vineyard obviously represents the Promised Land given to the people of Israel on the condition that they will produce the right spiritual fruit. 'The Torah', which Christians call 'the Pentateuch', is composed of the first five books of the Bible. These books make it clear to the Jewish people that the Promised Land is given to them on the condition that they remain faithful to God. They are warned that if they worship false gods that they will be exiled from the land (see Deuteronomy 28:15-25 and 28:58-68). No doubt Jesus' hearers would have been aware of these verses. The servants, sent to remind the tenants of the fruit they owed to the master of the vineyard, represent the Old Testament prophets sent to

remind the Israelites of the covenant they have with God. The master of
the vineyard represents God, and no doubt the son in the parable
represents Jesus himself. To this extent I, and other Christian Zionists,
fully agree with those who use this parable to support Replacement
Theology. However, in regard to the next symbol found in this allegory we
hold a completely different viewpoint. Proponents of Replacement
Theology teach that the tenants in this story represent the whole nation of
Israel. The nation which takes over from them, they suggest, is the Gentile
Church. They claim that this Gentile Church has produced much better
fruit than the nation of Israel.

I deeply disagree with this interpretation for several reasons. My
most important reason for rejecting this interpretation is that it does not
fit in with the reaction of the first hearers of this parable. Matthew makes
it clear that the corrupt religious leaders knew that Jesus referred to them
as the tenants which would murder the owner's son in verse 45. This being
the case, it is obvious that Jesus was not referring to the ordinary Jewish
people but rather to the corrupt religious leaders whom he referred to as
'blind guides'. Furthermore, as the story of the passion of Jesus unfolds, it
becomes most apparent that these religious leaders dared not try to arrest
Jesus during daylight hours. All these facts, reported in all four Gospels,
support the contention of those who oppose Replacement Theology. It
would be morally wrong and unloving for God to blame the whole Jewish
race for the behaviour of the religious leaders. It should also be
remembered that the Church remained predominantly Jewish for at least
twenty years after the death and resurrection of Jesus. For all these reasons
I suggest that it is wrong to infer that God has rejected the whole Jewish
race based on this parable. The nation that would inherit God's blessing
from the corrupt religious leaders is obviously the Church.

My contention is that the Church that is being referred to is both
Jew and Gentile, united together. I believe that it was never in God's
perfect will for the Church to become dominated by the Gentiles. Church
leaders, due to their arrogance, caused this to happen against God's
purpose. I also believe the Holy Spirit is seeking to sort out this imbalance
regarding the Gentile domination of the Church. To reverse this
imbalance he is leading many Christians to celebrate the Jewish roots of

their faith, celebrate God's feasts given to both Israel and his church, and Jews to find their wholeness in Jesus, their Messiah.

I rejoice at the formation of the Messianic movement both within Israel and across the nations. As a Zionist Christian, I see my own role as one of attempting to promote a proper understanding of our Jewish roots in Jesus our Messiah across the whole Body of Christ. This will, hopefully, create a wider level of appreciation of the debt we, as Christians, owe to the Jewish people amongst the Church, across all its denominational groupings. It will, hopefully, inspire other Christians to love the Jews and seek to combat the appalling level of misinformation regarding Israel found in our society, which has arisen from the biased news coverage we in the U.K. receive through our media.

The next argument used by the proponents of Replacement Theology, relates to the crowd of Jewish people that gathered at the Judgment Seat of Pilate, the Roman Governor of Judea. Supporters of Replacement Theology claim that the curse these Jewish men and women placed upon the Jews is still valid and effective today. An account of these events is found in Matthew 27:15-26. At first sight the dreadful words of this crowd, according to verse 25 of this chapter, seem to support what the advocates of Replacement Theology would want us to believe. They seem to support the theory that on this occasion the Jews brought God's curse upon them and their children forever.

However, when one looks into the background to this narrative and relates other scriptural references to this verse, the argument in favour of Replacement Theology is severely weakened. The first thing to note is that this crowd gathered at Pilate's Judgment Seat at 6 a.m. after a feast night. Most of the populace of Jerusalem would have been still asleep at this hour. The religious leaders deliberately planned to appear before Pilate at this early hour and paid for a mob to join them. They wanted to have Jesus tried and condemned to death before his many Jewish followers could gather and disrupt their plan. Fulfilling their plan meant that they had to try Jesus at night in the Sanhedrin, thus breaking their own rules as to how such trials should have been conducted. Thus this crowd could hardly be said to have been representative of the whole Jewish race. Even if this crowd had been representative of the Jewish race, Jesus' prayer for his enemies to receive his Father's forgiveness would have annulled any curse that the crowd had uttered against themselves and their children.

In Luke 23:34 it is recorded how Jesus asked for his Father's forgiveness for all involved in his death. Furthermore, before Jesus was even betrayed he had told his disciples that he would lay down his life to bring forgiveness to mankind. Jesus clearly stated that no human being could take his life from him (see John 10:18). It is therefore right to conclude that all mankind is responsible for the death of Jesus. The sin of each and every one of us made it necessary for Jesus to lay down his life for us. These biblical truths make the whole case for blaming the Jewish race for the death of Jesus look completely ridiculous. This is an issue of vital importance to the proponents of Replacement Theology. If it is clear that the Jewish people are not blameworthy for the rejection and death of Jesus, the question arises as to why God should reject them from their role as his 'chosen people' and replace them with the Gentile Church. For God to do this arbitrarily seems most unjust and unfair on his part. The question arises, "Is such a God loving and just?"

Another biblical reference quoted by proponents of Replacement Theology is found in 1 Peter 2:9-10. In this passage Peter speaks of Gentile believers becoming a chosen people because of their faith in Jesus. In verse 10 he makes it clear that these believers were once not chosen by God. Proponents of Replacement Theology claim that Peter is suggesting that these Gentiles had replaced the Jews in becoming God's chosen people. This suggestion is in no way made explicit in these verses. Peter never states that the Jews have in any way been replaced by the Gentiles. Christian Zionists would fully accept the fact that Gentile Christians have been accepted as a chosen people because of their faith in Jesus. However, they reject the idea that their acceptance through adoption into this role implies that the Jews have been rejected from this role. It is logical to accept the concept of the Jews still remaining in their role and the Gentiles being accepted in the role of a chosen people alongside them.

In my analysis of the other arguments of the supporters of Replacement Theology I will often be referring to an article written by Clarence Wagner Jr. In his article 'The Error of Replacement Theology' Wagner pays great detail to the arguments put forward by supporters of

Replacement Theology and confounds their arguments in a very concise and convincing manner. The first argument he deals with relates to Galatians 3:29. In this verse Apostle Paul refers to believers in Jesus being spiritually the sons of Abraham.

Supporters of Replacement Theology have argued that this verse suggests that Christians have now taken over the role the Jews had as the natural seeds of Abraham. However, this verse only implies that Gentile Christians have been adopted into this role alongside the natural sons - not as a replacement for them. Wagner concludes:

> *This verse simply joins us Gentile Christians to what God has already started with Israel.*

Bible verses which support the concept that God's covenant with Israel is a permanent one are numerous. Paul wrote in Romans 11:1 that God had not rejected the Jews at all and, indeed, would never do so. Even in Deuteronomy chapter 32, where the Israelites are warned that their sin will bring terrible suffering upon them and that they would be scattered among the nations, there is no suggestion made that God would remove them from their role as the chosen people. Rather in verses 36-43 of this chapter there come God's promise of restoration to Israel and his promise to punish their enemies. In Jeremiah 31:35-37 God makes it abundantly clear that Israel will be preserved by him as a nation as long as the fixed ordinances of creation remain. He even promises never to "cast them off" regardless of how much they sin against him. Through the prophet Isaiah, God makes similar promises regarding the Israelites. In Isaiah 49:3-7 promises are made regarding them never being swept away, that kings and princes will prostrate themselves before them and that God will bring salvation through them to the ends of the earth. In chapter 62 God makes it clear that through the Jewish inhabitants of Jerusalem God will be glorified throughout all nations. He also promises to vindicate the Jews and impart his righteousness to them. In Malachi 3:6 God makes it clear that in the same way that he never changes, the natural sons of Jacob will never be consumed and destroyed by the nations.

Supporters of Replacement Theology claim that Romans 4:13 suggests that the Church, not Israel, now inherits the whole world due to

their faith in Jesus. In response to this claim I would suggest that those
who make it are inferring far too much from what is actually said.
Nowhere in this verse is the word 'Church' mentioned. It never suggests
that the Jews are excluded from the fulfilment of this promise. All that it
suggests is that both Gentiles and the natural offspring of Abraham, the
Jews, inherit the world due to their faith. Surely it is through the faith of
Jewish believers in Jesus that all the nations have been blessed through the
proclamation of the gospel.

Some supporters of Replacement Theology suggest Malachi 1:11
infers that the nation of Israel was only the seed of the future church
which now incorporates all nations. Again these brethren infer far too
much from this verse. Malachi makes it known that through the Jews God
will make himself known to the ends of the earth. He in no way states that
when this happens the Jews will cease to be the 'chosen people'. Later in
his book Malachi makes it clear that God promises that due to his
unchanging nature the sons of Jacob (the Jewish people) are not
consumed (see Malachi 3:6). Thus this verse claims that God is constantly
linked to his covenant with the Jewish people, based upon his unchanging
nature.

The most ridiculous claim of some of the advocates of Replacement
Theology is that the symbol of the olive tree in Romans chapter 11 now
stands for 'the Church'. Wagner concludes:

> *This claim is the most outrageous because this passage clearly shows that
> we Gentiles are the 'wild olive branches', who get our life from being
> grafted into the olive tree. The tree represents the covenants, promises and
> hopes of Israel (Ephesians 2:v12), rooted in the Messiah and fed by the
> sap, which represents the Holy Spirit, giving life to the Jews (the natural
> branches) and the Gentiles alike. We, Gentiles, are told to remember that
> the olive tree holds us up and NOT to be arrogant or boast against the
> natural branches because they can be grafted in again. The olive tree is
> NOT the Church. We are simply grafted into God's plan that preceded
> us for over 2,000 years.*

When reading Paul's words in Romans chapter 11 it seems almost
unbelievable that someone could interpret the symbol of the olive tree as

representing the Church. The conclusion runs completely opposite to what Paul states in Romans chapters 9, 10 and 11. His theme throughout these chapters is that God has not, and never will, cast the natural descendants of the patriarchs (Abraham, Isaac and Jacob) aside. He admits some of them have been removed from the olive tree through unbelief but states that God will never break his covenant with the patriarchs. God honours his covenant with them regardless of the lack of faithfulness on the part of some of their natural descendants.

Another remarkable claim made by some of the advocates of Replacement Theology is that all the promises of the Old Testament which were made to Israel have now become the property of the Christian church. In support of their claim they quote 2 Corinthians 1:20. They suggest that this verse implies that every promise of God is now fulfilled in us as Christian believers. Again, this verse does not explicitly suggest that the Church has taken the place of the Jewish people in the purposes of God. The promise of God preserving Israel as a nation found in Jeremiah chapter 31 surely cannot be transferred to the Church. The Church, by its very nature, is international with members belonging to racial groups spanning every continent. Yet, as we have seen, this divine promise applies as long as creation's ordinances exist. Surely God cannot contradict himself in such a blatant manner and be considered to be ethically righteous and trustworthy. Wagner states the case against the false interpretation of the biblical passages by the advocates of Replacement Theology in a very succinct manner:

> ...*no promise to Israel and the Jewish people in the Bible is figurative, nor can they be relegated to the Church alone. The promises and covenants are literal, many of them are everlasting, and we Christians can participate in them as part of our rebirth, not in that we took them over to the exclusion of Israel.*

How can you apply God's promises to Israel in Isaiah chapter 49 to the Church? In this chapter God promises (in verse 22) that he will call for the Gentiles to help the Jewish exiles back to the land of Israel after they have been scattered across the nations to the ends of the earth. It might be suggested that this prophecy speaks of the restoration of the Jews back to their land after the Babylonian exile; however, major problems then arise in matching the verses with the historical events that actually took place. The end of the exile only involved the Jews returning home from the north and, other than King Cyrus, the Gentiles were not at all involved in this process. Gentiles never carried Jewish children in their arms at the end of this exile. These details have only been fulfilled in the recent return of the Jewish people to the modern State of Israel.

Applying this prophecy to the Church is even more problematic. I cannot for one moment think how the members have been re-gathered to a geographical homeland or how Gentiles have been involved in carrying Christian children on their shoulders. How on earth could this promise be applied in any sense to the Church? How would Replacement Theology apply the prophecies of Zechariah to the Church, particularly Zechariah 13:1-6 and 14:1-19. It seems impossible for such prophecies to have any real fulfilment unless they are fulfilled in the context of the Jewish people and the State of Israel. In order to spiritualise these biblical prophecies the proponents of Replacement Theology would need to do spiritual gymnastics with them.

At this point it seems right to highlight a great inconsistency in the way that advocates of Replacement Theology selectively ascribe Old Testament promises (given to Israel) as given to the Church. If the promises Israel received dependant upon their obedience should now be spiritualised as given to the Church, why should the same not apply for the curses resulting from disobedience? Simple logic suggests that this *should* be the case. I have not yet read of any advocate of Replacement Theology willing to apply this simple logic. Rather they are happy to ascribe to the Jewish people the curses for disobedience.

Has the Church throughout the ages been obedient to the teachings of our Saviour Jesus? I think most honest observers would agree with me in saying that the Church has far too often failed to do this. The sins of arrogance and bigotry have far too often caused those who have professed to be followers to live lives which fall terribly short of the standard set for them in the teaching of Jesus. Gandhi, the great prophet of non-violence, said that although he greatly admired Jesus and his teachings, he did not want to become a Christian because of the hypocrisy of far too many

Christians who he had met. In the light of the sad history of the Church, I believe it is inappropriate for Christians to claim that the Church has been far more faithful to God than the nation of Israel had been. Yet this is a claim held.

One of the passages quoted by a few proponents of Replacement Theology is found in Revelation 2:8-10. Here Jesus refers to a group of Jews as a 'synagogue of Satan'. Some extreme supporters of Replacement Theology have attempted to use this passage to claim that Jewish synagogues have been taken over by the demonic. I must point out that only this one synagogue is referred to in this way. This one synagogue allowed the sins of arrogance and bigotry to so dominate its members that they became the unwitting tools through which Satan could work. This one example cannot be legitimately used to suggest that all synagogues have succumbed to the same level of moral wickedness. I would also ask the question: how many churches have allowed the sins of arrogance and bigotry to so dominate their members that they have become the unwitting agents of evil through which Satan has been able to fulfil his wicked plans?

One of the tactics of some of the proponents of Replacement Theology has been to misrepresent the beliefs of Zionist Christians. Stephen Sizer, in his book 'Christian Zionism' suggests that Christian Zionists seek to use their influence to get Israel to attack her Arab neighbours, to enlarge her territory through force of arms and to get the western nations to back this action. He warns that their influence could help to promote terrible bloodshed and precipitate another world war leading to Armageddon. He clearly implies that all Christian Zionists desire war and not peace in the Middle East. He believes that Christian Zionists want to help God in bringing about this conflict, to help speed the fulfilment of biblical prophecy and thus the Second Coming of Jesus.

My first observation in answering this point is that the State of Israel has no desire to engage in wars to extend her borders. In fact the Israeli Government has surrendered territory for peace. My second point is the fact that Christian Zionists who believe that Israel will again receive back all the territory promised to the Patriarchs believe that this will be brought about by God's intervention, not by Israel launching an invasion of her neighbours.

Most Christian Zionists believe that Israel should not surrender any more land for peace because all previous attempts at following this strategy have failed to bring peace. They might also refer to the fact that both Hamas and Fatah (the main political parties of the Palestinians) are committed to the destruction of the State of Israel and not peaceful co-existence. Rather than praying for Israel to launch territorial expansion, most Christian Zionists pray for an end to conflict but one which allows Israel to have secure borders and an end to acts of terror launched against her citizens. I believe that Stephen Sizer is wrong to suggest that the only alternative to Replacement Theology is a militant Christian Zionism which is hell-bent on bringing about mass slaughter in the Middle East and potential Armageddon to the world. Such Christian Zionists are largely a figment of his imagination. I believe that this argument is not only unfair but also unconvincing once one examines the facts of the case they put forward. Derek White, in his pamphlet 'Christian Zionism', states:

> *Christian Zionism is not a belief that everything Israel does today carries divine sanction, nor that her leaders at any time carry divine authority outside that defined in Romans chapter 13:1-6. It is not a rejection of the Arab people, especially those who live in the land of Israel. It is not a belief that the ONLY criterion of divine judgment on nations and individuals is their attitude to the treatment of the Jews.*

I would add to this that most Christian Zionists want to see fairness in our media when presenting the conflict between Israel and Palestinians. Few Christian Zionists would condone the deliberate violation of Palestinian human rights. Being favourable to the Jewish people and recognising the debt that we as Christians owe to them does not logically mean that one must hate Arabs. It does not mean that one desires that the State of Israel should seek to extend its borders by military means.

Those professing to be Palestinians already form the majority of the population of the Arab State of Jordan. This fact seems to be little known amongst those who espouse the Palestinian cause. This surely indicates that the Palestinians have plenty of land to use as their own in this state without needing to make further territorial claims upon the territory of Israel. Jordan is a much larger country than Israel. However, Jordan is ruled by a dictatorial Arab monarch who represses most of his people, including those who profess to be Palestinians. He does not want to integrate an even larger Palestinian populace in Jordan. This also explains why Jordan has never asked for the land on the West Bank of the River Jordan to again be brought under Jordanian control. His predecessor has had his security forces kill more Palestinians than have ever died as a result of their conflict with Israel. Again this is another fact that Palestinian supporters in the west seem unaware of. Why didn't the rest of the world complain when Jordanian forces massacred and exiled so many Palestinians? The answer is that they did not want to upset the Arab oil sheiks. It was not in their national interests to speak out.

Another argument put forward by Stephen Sizer concerns the ethical dimension of conflict between Israel and the Palestinians. Stephen Sizer quotes the Resolution 3379 of the United Nations General Assembly as a proof that Israel's actions towards the Palestinian people amounts to "a form of racism and racial discrimination". He implies that Christian Zionists are obviously being unethical if they show any support for the State of Israel. Underlying his conclusion that the Israelis have behaved unethically is his belief that the Jewish people have been replaced by the Christian church in their role as the chosen people. This is his reason for suggesting that the Jewish people have no moral right to have possession of the land which now forms the State of Israel. Stephen Sizer writes:

> *God's mission for Israel to the world is summed up in the person and ministry of Jesus Christ who fulfilled God's purposes for Israel. He did this by creating out of two peoples- Jews and Gentiles- one people whose Promised Land is no longer a piece of real estate in the Middle East, but a new Heaven and a new Earth, which comes into existence when he comes again.*[12]

My first response to this argument is to question his choice of the United Nations as the moral arbiter regarding the Israeli-Palestinian

---

[12] www.christianzionism.org

conflict. As I suggested in my introduction, the very composition of the General Assembly means that the representatives of the nations will vote for motions which favour their national self-interest, not what is morally right or wrong. I have no doubt that the particular vote that Sizer refers to was motivated by national representatives wanting to please the Arab oil-rich states rather than making ethical statements of what is truly moral or immoral regarding this issue.

My question is simply: how ethical is the United Nations in fulfilling its roles of protecting vulnerable people from the actions of dictators and tyrants and keeping world peace? I suggest that this body has largely failed to act ethically in regard to these roles. As illustrations of this contention, I would cite the U.N.'s failure to do anything to stop the policy of genocide launched by the majority tribe against the minority tribe in Rwanda. In regard to this conflict the U.N. already had a military force in the country at the time. No attempt was made to radically increase the number of peacekeepers in the country to halt the genocide which had started. The principle of not intervening in the internal affairs of this state was upheld - at tremendous cost to the thousands of innocent people who were slaughtered for no other reason than the tribe which they were born into. In the same way, due to China's unlimited support for the dictatorial regime of Robert Mugabe, the U.N. has allowed thousands of innocent Zimbabweans to be tortured and murdered by his regime. Hardly a murmur of protest has arisen in the U.N. about this issue. Mugabe's regime has transformed this beautiful country from its role as the bread-basket of Southern Africa to the basket-case of Southern Africa. The U.N. has done nothing to halt this process. Only due to intense pressure from Britain and France was anything done to stop the slaughter in Libya. Some of the nations on the Security Council of the U.N. were highly reluctant to endorse this action which undoubtedly saved the lives of thousands of people. Action to stop the bloodshed occurred at the last possible moment. Today it is reasonable to ask the question as to why the U.N. seems so reluctant to do anything to end the slaughter of innocent people by the dictatorial regime of Assad in Syria. These are only some of the instances which can be referred to as evidence of the U.N.'s failure to uphold human rights and prevent tyranny in the world today. Given the undoubted failure of the United Nations to uphold morality among the nations, why is Stephen Sizer so keen to quote U.N. resolutions as evidence of immorality exhibited by the State of Israel?

Can an agency as morally corrupt as the United Nations define what is morally right or wrong? I am certainly not a racist but support the State of Israel's right of self-determination and of self-defence. I am saddened by the slaughter of innocent Arabs whenever this occurs. I am appalled at the slaughter of innocent protesters presently taking place in Syria. The State of Israel cannot be described as being inherently racist. How can this be the case when this state has many Arab citizens who live within its borders as equals to the Jewish citizens living within it? There are currently many Arab members of the Jewish parliament and the Israelis have tried giving the Palestinians land for peace with no success whatsoever. I believe that God has remained faithful to his promises in the Scriptures regarding the Jewish people being re-gathered to their land. I believe that having a piece of real estate in the land of Israel is vital to the Jewish people. There they can feel that they have a land in which they belong. Given the cruel treatment and social exclusion which they have suffered down the centuries this is perfectly understandable. I also believe that God in his providence has worked through the affairs of mankind to bring about this restoration of the Jewish people to their land which he promised to their ancestors. Perhaps if the advocates of Replacement Theology would seriously study the catalogue of Jewish suffering down the centuries they would become far more sympathetic to the Jewish people and less inclined to always side with their enemies. Maybe they would cease to be so uncritical of the rhetoric of militant Arabs who desire to wipe out all Jews living in the land of Israel.

The doctrine of Replacement Theology has blinded its advocates to the reality of biblical prophecies being fulfilled regarding the rebirth of the State of Israel in 1948. I believe that it is their spiritual blindness that has caused these Christian believers to be so unaware of the realities taking place in the Middle East. Christian Zionists are not having a great influence over their governments regarding foreign policy in relation to the State of Israel.

Combating the Arguments used by those who Promote and Defend the Doctrine of Replacement Theology

Mark Woods, an advocate of Replacement Theology, wrote in the Baptist Times of December 18th 2008:

Particularly in the U.S., these Christian Zionist organizations, which believe in the return of the Jews to the Holy Land as a result of prophecy, have huge influence both theologically and politically.

I agree entirely with the sentiment expressed by the author of 'Wildolive' - Christian Zionism:

Oh that we did, instead of being a despised and ignored minority.

The rulings of the Church councils, which were by nature anti-Jewish and were to a great extent inspired by the doctrine of Replacement Theology, labelled those who desired to celebrate the Jewishness of Jesus as heretical. They were accused of being Judaizers. I believe that this charge against clerics and lay-people who are sympathetic towards the Jewish people is most unfair. Christian Zionists do not want Gentiles to get circumcised, live in accordance with Jewish customs and eat 'kosher' food. These were the teachings of the Judaizers which were so rebuked by the apostle Paul. Rather we wish to support the Jewish people and combat the wrong impressions of Israel put forward by our media. We wish to celebrate the biblical feasts given by God to both Israel and the Church. We wish to encourage Jews to be fulfilled in Jesus, their Messiah, without having to give up their Jewish culture.

I like to see Jews worship God in their traditional dress, choose to continue circumcising their children as Messianic Jews and choose to continue eating 'kosher' foods. It is their right to do so. I reject the claim that I am trying to turn Gentiles into Jews. I would discourage any Gentile believers seeking to be circumcised for religious reasons, as their actions would run completely contrary to the decision of the Jerusalem council regarding this issue in Acts 15. They would also run completely contrary to Apostle Paul's instructions in his Letter to the Galatians. I would also dissuade anyone trying to impose the eating of 'kosher' foods upon Gentile believers because Jesus declared all foods clean in Mark 7:14-23. Instead I am trying to undo the negative influence of anti-Jewishness upon the Church in general by exposing the doctrine of Replacement Theology as an anti-biblical, unjust teaching. With a humble attitude of servanthood believers in Jesus can then approach non-Messianic Jews and declare to them, "Behold your God." (See Isaiah 52:7-11). I believe that believers need to cry many tears of repentance over how many sections of the Church have treated the Jewish people over the centuries. I believe that only a fresh wave of God's love, brought into the Church by believers repenting of the evil done in the name of Jesus to the Jews, will remove the poison of Replacement Theology from the pot. Only then will multiple thousands of Jews embrace Jesus as their true Messiah, thus fulfilling the words of Apostle Paul in Romans 11:26-27.

The New Direction of Replacement Theology in the 20th and 21st Centuries

As we have seen, historically, Replacement Theology arose as a theological response to explain why many Jewish people had failed to respond positively to the gospel. It also provided a way to distance the new religion of Christianity from its Jewish roots when it became expedient to do so (when the Roman Emperors had turned against Judaism.) Gentile arrogance and boastfulness played a major role in the development of this doctrine during the times of the Church Fathers.

From the establishment of the State of Israel in 1948, advocates of Replacement Theology have increasingly sided with the Palestinian cause in opposition to the re-establishment of the Jewish state. They see themselves as standing up against Jewish oppression of the Palestinian people. Some Palestinian leaders have sought to deny the Jewishness of Jesus and have presented him as a persecuted Palestinian. This is, indeed, an amazing claim to make. It is clear that Jesus identified himself as belonging to the Jewish race. In his conversation with the Samaritan woman in John chapter 4 Jesus referred to himself as belonging to the line of Israel. In John 4:22 Jesus stated, "We Jews know whom we worship."

At no point in any of the gospels did Jesus refer to himself as a 'Palestinian'. For these reasons it is simply historically wrong for these Palestinians to refer to Jesus as a persecuted Palestinian. Indeed, since Palestine was derived from the word 'Philistine', the old enemy of the Jewish people that was completely defeated during the reign of King David, no Jew, Arab or Samaritan would have ever called themselves Palestinians at the time of Jesus. There is little doubt that the Romans called the land of Israel Palestine as an insult to the Jewish people whom they had defeated militarily and as a reminder of the power of the new conquerors.

Indeed it is true to say that no independent country called Palestine has ever existed. It was the name conquerors gave to this area when they had acquired it by military means. The so-called 'occupied territories' of the West Bank and Gaza were never independent territories called Palestine, under the control of the Palestinian people. Rather, prior to the

Six Day War in 1967, the West Bank belonged to the Kingdom of Jordan and the Gaza belonged to Egypt. Yet, despite all this evidence to the contrary, prominent Palestinians have persisted in the claim that Jesus was a persecuted Palestinian. Dr. Paul Wilkinson, in his article "'Prophets who Prophesy Lies in my Name": Christian Palestinianism and the Anti-Israel Crusade', cites clear examples of prominent Palestinian leaders making these claims. He quotes Palestinian Media Watch as providing the following examples:

> *...religious leader Muhammad Hussain has suggested that Jesus and Mary were 'Palestinians par excellence'.*

Author Shamih Ghanadreh when interviewed on Palestinian T.V. asserted that Jesus was the first Palestinian martyr, or 'shahid'. Mustafa Barghouti, an influential leader within the Palestinian Authority, made a similar claim in December 2009, when he described Jesus as "the first Palestinian to be tortured in this land." The sad thing is that Christian ministers who actively support and advocate Replacement Theology have done nothing at all to distance themselves from these false claims regarding the one they profess to be the Son of God.

In fact, Naim Ateek, an Anglican priest and founder of the Palestinian Ecumenical Liberation Theology Centre, seems to openly support this historically inaccurate view of Jesus. In his book 'A Palestinian Christian Cry for Reconciliation' (2008), he claims:

> *In many ways a Palestinian theology of liberation has re-established the balance between Christ's two natures - his divinity and his humanity. Palestinian liberation theology focuses on the humanity of Jesus of Nazareth, who was a Palestinian living under an occupation.*

In his Easter message preached on the 9th April 2001, Ateek said:

> *Here in Palestine Jesus is again walking down the Via Dolorosa. Jesus is the powerless Palestinian humiliated at the checkpoint, the woman trying to get through to the hospital for treatment, the young man whose dignity is trampled, the young student who cannot get to the university to*

study, the unemployed father who needs to find bread to feed his family ... In this season of Lent, it seems to many of us that Jesus is on the cross again with thousands of crucified Palestinians around him. It only takes people of insight to see the hundreds of thousands of crosses throughout the land, Palestinian men, women and children being crucified. Palestine has become one huge Golgotha. The Israeli government crucifixion system is working daily.

The main thing that Ateek missed out in his sermon is the fact that it is the Palestinian leaders that have brought about the need for such checkpoints by supporting terror attacks on Israeli citizens - both Jews and Arabs alike. If these terror attacks were to permanently cease then the Israelis would no longer erect and man these checkpoints. He also failed to state the well-known fact that if all the money which had been given in aid to the Palestinian Authority had been used to boost the economy and relieve poverty then the economic welfare of its citizens would be markedly improved. Sadly, vast quantities of aid money has been stolen by corrupt Palestinian officials or spent on explosives to blow up Israeli citizens. I am sure Jesus' heart is moved to compassion over the suffering of the ordinary Palestinian people. I believe that all Christians should be saddened about their suffering.

Yet, the fact remains that the Palestinian leadership, both Fatah and Hamas, is largely to blame for this suffering, not the Israeli government. To equate their suffering with the terrible sufferings of Jesus, the Sinless One, seems to me to be a seriously wrong analogy. Perhaps viewing again the film 'The Passion of the Christ' might help Rev. Ateek to understand just how much Jesus suffered willingly for us all to redeem us from sin. The fact that Ateek had the freedom to express these views to a congregation in Jerusalem, an area under Israeli administration, is remarkable proof of how democratic and tolerant the Israeli government is in regard to its treatment of Palestinian activists. There are few countries in the Arab world where political opponents of the state are allowed freedom of speech to such an extent as that allowed in the State of Israel. Had Rev. Ateek preached a sermon critical of the Syrian government within Syria he would have been detained at best, or at worst he would have disappeared without trace.

Is there Death in the Pot?

The question obviously arises: how have so many Christians come to a level of devotion to the Palestinian cause whilst being so opposed to the existence of the State of Israel? No doubt part of the answer to this question is that so many Christians have been subtly influenced to believe the worst about the Jewish people due to the impact of Replacement Theology. The concept that the Jews are mistreating the Palestinians is put forward by the biased news reporting arising from much of the western media. In addition to this all the Arab groups fighting Israel are good at manipulating situations in such a way as to present the Jewish people in a bad light in the eyes of the media.

It is well known, for example, that Hamas fighters firing rockets into southern Israel have deliberately fired them from residential areas. Such a battle strategy is obviously calculated to expose Palestinian civilians to enemy fire. The aim is, no doubt, to win the propaganda battle at the cost of the lives of ordinary Palestinian citizens. The Palestinian fighters know that Israeli forces will fire back at the areas from which the rockets are fired, in the process killing and injuring these civilians. The Hamas regime is then able to point to the supposed cruelty of the Israeli forces. Similar strategies have been used by Fatah in the past. It is also well known that Palestinian fighters have fired on Israeli soldiers from behind ordinary Palestinian women and children protesters. They obviously want these Israelis to shoot back, killing and injuring civilians. They are then able to use these casualties for propaganda purposes against the Israelis. When many Christians have witnessed such events on the news they have concluded that the Israelis rather than the Palestinian leaders are to blame for these events. They have completely failed to reflect upon why so many Palestinian civilians have been killed or injured during the conflict with the Israelis and have been quick to conclude that the Zionist government of Israel is to blame entirely for these casualties.

Another factor leading to many Christians actively siding with the Palestinians has been the failure of the World Council of Churches to adopt a neutral stance in regard to the Arab-Israeli conflict. From its very inception in August 1948 the World Council of Churches (W.C.C.) has been one-sided. It has consistently sided with the Arabs. No doubt the fact that so many founders of this movement have arisen from among the advocates of Replacement Theology explains, to a great extent, this obvious bias. The W.C.C. has rightly been a platform for Christian Arabs to express their viewpoints regarding the Palestinian-Israeli conflict. However, neither representatives of the Israelis nor Christian Zionists have been invited to express their viewpoints. The fact that the W.C.C. has adopted such an anti-Israeli, pro-Palestinian position has given the Palestinian cause a great level of legitimacy in the eyes of many ordinary Christians.

The formation of Sabeel Palestinian Ecumenical Liberation Theology Centre, based in Jerusalem, in 1994 has given Christians desiring to recruit other Christians to the cause of 'Palestinian liberation' a well-resourced organization through which to operate. This organization has set up 'International Friends of Sabeel' in the U.S.A, Canada, the United Kingdom, Ireland, Scandinavia and Oceana. Rev. Naim Ateek has been a very eloquent spokesman for the organization. It has been consistently backed and given world-wide legitimacy by the W.C.C. We Christian Zionists have lacked such a well-respected body to co-ordinate our efforts at answering the propaganda of this group. I believe that many Christians are very ill-informed regarding the Palestinian-Israeli conflict and, therefore, are unable to evaluate the deeper issues underlying this conflict.

Far too many Christians, I believe, trust the advice given to them by their ministers or priests without thinking issues through for themselves. Many Christians have eagerly joined the boycott of Israeli goods in protest at the alleged racist actions of the State of Israel without making any real attempt at understanding what is really taking place in the Middle East. Many of these sincere Christian believers have had little in-depth biblical knowledge upon which to genuinely evaluate the moral issues arising from the Palestinian-Israeli conflict. I believe these folk are being misled. These actions by people perceived to represent the whole Christian community cause great pain to the Jewish people. My Jewish friend, the late Russell Cohen, would often express to me the frustration and hurt he felt over this biased anti-Jewish behaviour on the part of so many Christian believers. Martyn, our dear Messianic Jewish man, still expresses to me his sorrow regarding the failure of so many Christians to have any real understanding of what is really taking place in Israel. I believe that

Christian Zionists need to become far more vocal in defending what we believe to be the truth regarding events in the Middle East. We need to confront the teaching of Replacement Theology head on. In order to do this we all need to be aware of the issues raised by its proponents. We need to be able to offer biblical answers that relate to these issues. We also need to become aware of how these leaders follow the mode of interpreting the Bible in such a non-literalist way that they spiritualise so many Bible passages that relate to Israel in both the Old and New Testaments.

Bat Ye'or has summarised the impact that the pro-Palestinian clergy are having on the wider church and has suggested that they themselves are being manipulated by Muslim extremists in her book 'Eurabia':

> *The Islamization of the Jewish sources of Christianity, disseminated through European Islamophile church networks, plays into the hands of Muslims, eager to co-opt Christianity and instrumentalize Christians as partners in their struggle against Israel.*

Rev. Dr. Stephen Sizer is a prominent Anglican clergyman who advocates Replacement Theology. Photographs of him in Iran, one of the most anti-Israeli, militant Arab states, do not bring any comfort to those of us who believe our fellow Christians are being manipulated by Arab dictators like President Ahmadinejad. One picture on his website shows him behind a small portrait of Ayatollah Khomeini, the architect of the Iranian revolution. In October 2007, whilst visiting Iran, Stephen Sizer spoke out, blaming Israel as the sole cause of all the conflict which is taking place in the Middle East.

Having listened to this dear brother speaking via the internet I do not for one moment doubt his sincerity. I believe he genuinely wants peace to come to the Middle East. If only the Muslim extremists, so set on the destruction of the State of Israel, were so sincere in their motives. If only the Palestinian leaders were willing to reach a genuine peace deal with the State of Israel that gave the Jewish people the certainty of peace and security that they so long for. Looking at the fight for genuine freedom and democracy that became apparent in the springtime of 2011 and how these hopes are fading in Libya due to divisions among the anti-Gaddaffi coalition, and in Egypt due to the slow pace of reform, it does not give one reason for genuine hope that a truly democratic, peaceful Palestinian State can be born.

The bitter rivalry between the two Palestinian movements, the oppression and human rights abuses which have occurred in the Palestinian Authority areas and the undoubted corruption of past and present Palestinian leaders, leaves even less hope of this taking place. If the State of Israel were to collapse, anarchy and mass destruction would be the outcome for both Jews and Arabs living in this area. The terrible scenes we saw in the Lebanese civil war and that we are now witnessing in Iraq, as the Sunni and Shi'ite factions of Islam battle for ascendency, would be repeated as Hamas and Fatah would fight a bitter civil war over which of them would govern the new Palestine. Thankfully, I believe recent history and biblical prophecy indicate the fact that God will not permit this to take place.

As a minister of religion, with a keen interest in Islamic history and Church history and historical facts concerning the intolerance and in-fighting that adherents of both religions have constantly engaged in, it does not leave me with much hope that human beings will ever achieve a permanent peace in the Middle East. I do not believe that the Israelis are to blame for the recurrent instability in the region. In effect, if the State of Israel did not exist, the Arab nations in the Middle East would still be plagued by internal strife and would be battling each other over which of them would be dominant in the region.

The main cause of the failure of the peace process is due to the insistence of the Palestinians that Jerusalem must be divided between Israel and themselves. No Israeli government would agree to such a proposal as it would be so unpopular among Jewish voters. The failure of Hamas to recognise the right of the State of Israel to exist is another serious barrier to the resumption of the peace process. There is also the recognition among many Israelis that they have already given up so much land in order to achieve peace and live within secure borders, but have received back nothing but trouble from the Palestinian factions. Hamas' use of the Gaza Strip to fire rockets into southern Israel has done absolutely nothing to cause the Israeli public or the Israeli government to have any confidence in the peace process. Lastly, the internal conflict plaguing both of Israel's Arab neighbours, Egypt and Syria, adds to the feeling of uncertainty within Israel, making the Israeli government reluctant to enter a new phase of the peace process until they have a greater degree of certainty as to who will be present at such negotiations. The role of Egypt within the peace process is absolutely critical if the negotiations are to start again.

The other issue which needs to be raised is that some supporters of the Palestinians appear to over-estimate the influence of Christian Zionists upon the United States government and foreign policy. The U.S.A. has backed Israel in the United Nations. On occasions the U.S.A. has used its power of veto to block anti-Israeli resolutions from being passed by the Security Council. However, the influence of Christian Zionists is not the determining factor securing this U.S. government action. The U.S.A. sees Israel as a valuable force for stability in the Middle East and an ally in the fight against Islamic terrorism. American politicians fear that the collapse of Israel could lead to the formation of an extremist Palestinian state or, even worse, a divided Palestinian state fighting a bitter civil war, which might cause the neighbouring Arab states to intervene and fight each other. These strategic factors, along with a large Jewish electorate within the U.S.A., have been the determinant factors guiding U.S. foreign policy. These have been the reasons why Britain and the U.S.A. have supported Israel economically. The fact that Israel is the only functioning democracy in the region has inclined Britain, the U.S.A. and other Western Governments to quietly back the continuation of the State of Israel.

Other Christian supporters of the Palestinian cause have made some ridiculous claims regarding the motivation of Christian Zionists as to why they support the Israelis. Naim Ateek, in his book 'Challenging Christian Zionism' suggests:

> *Christian Zionists want the Jewish people to be brought back to the land of Israel in order for them to be annihilated or converted to the Christian faith.*

Although many Christian Zionists believe that there will be a revival in Israel, they choose to support the Jewish people in returning to Israel because they believe they are helping them to have freedom and safety in their land. They also believe that God has called the Gentile Christians to show their appreciation to the Jewish people for what they contributed to the spiritual blessing of mankind. By helping the Jewish people they are fulfilling God's call to help them. Most Christian Zionists do not believe that the nation of Israel is about to be wiped out. They believe that a generation of Jewish people will freely choose to embrace Jesus as their Messiah in fulfilment of the prophecy of Zechariah chapter 12. No Christian Zionist will claim that they know exactly when this prophecy will be fulfilled. Most Christian Zionists believe that the prophetic passages of the Bible arise out of God's foreknowledge of future events. They do not believe that God manipulates human free will in order to bring about the fulfilment of these prophecies. They are motivated by God's love for the Jewish people, not from the ulterior motive of trying to 'convert' them. Most Christian Zionists recognise, along with other evangelical Christians, that conversion comes as a result of the work of the Holy Spirit and the operation of human free will in choosing to receive God's undeserved grace and the gift of his salvation.

Mitri Raheb, pastor of the Evangelical Lutheran Christmas Church in Bethlehem, has suggested that Christian Zionists do not support the Palestinian cause because they want to support success. They see Palestinians as losers (of wars). This is perhaps the worst suggestion made by the pro-Palestinian lobby regarding the motivation of Christian Zionists. Christian Zionists obviously support the Jewish people for what they perceive as scriptural reasons, not because Israel wins wars. They oppose the Palestinian leadership and their anti-Jewish policies, not the Palestinian people. They believe that the suffering of the Palestinian people is largely to be blamed upon the wrong policies of their leaders, not the necessary policies that the Israeli government has had to develop to protect their citizens from the Palestinian threat of terrorism.

Most recently there has been an attempt on the part of some of the pro-Palestinian advocates of Replacement Theology to rebrand their teaching as 'fulfilment theology'. Paul Wilkinson, in his article '"Prophets who Prophesy Lies in my Name": Christian Palestinianism and the anti-Israel Crusade', suggests:

...Christian Palestinianists have tried, and failed, to rebrand their Replacement Theology as Fulfilment Theology. Their basic assertion is ... that Jesus fulfilled all the promises relating to the return of the Jewish people to the Land.

He then quotes the words of Colin Chapman, a leading member of the pro-Palestinian lobby and leading advocate of Replacement Theology. Colin Chapman wrote in his book 'Whose Promised Land?' the following words:

The New Testament writers ceased to look forward to a literal fulfilment of Old Testament prophecies of the return to the land and a restored Jewish state. The one and only fulfilment of all the promises and prophecies was already before their eyes in the person of Jesus.

I find this to be an incredible statement for any Christian theologian to make. I cannot see how prophecies about Jewish people returning to a physical land and being helped by Gentiles to do so can be fulfilled in some non-physical way in the person of Jesus. I would really like Colin Chapman to explain to me in simple English what he means. To me he is writing fine-sounding words that have no credible meaning. The fact that Jesus himself made a physical prophecy about the future of a physical Jerusalem suggests that the arguments of this brother are unfounded.

According to Luke's Gospel, Jesus made a clear prediction concerning the future of the city of Jerusalem. He told that Jerusalem would come under the control of Gentiles for many years, and they would trample on its streets throughout those many years. However, he went on to say that the times of the Gentiles would eventually come to an end. He implied then that control of Jerusalem would once again return to the Jewish people (see Luke 21:24). Surely this prediction of Jesus was fulfilled in 1967 when Jerusalem was taken over by the State of Israel. The fact that Jesus made predictions about future events regarding 20th century Israel clearly implies that God is still involved with the events affecting both the Jewish people and their land. This surely contradicts the assertions of the advocates of Replacement Theology that God is finished with the Jewish people.

One of the most controversial aspects of the theology expressed by the pro-Palestinian lobby of Christian theologians is their attitude towards the interpretation of scriptural passages. They suggest that if a passage of scripture fits in with their personal understanding of God then it is acceptable; if not they are to regard it as unacceptable and having no authority.

Naim Ateek outlined this view of how to interpret the Bible in his book 'Justice and only Justice'. He wrote:

> *When confronted by a difficult passage in the Bible ... one needs to ask a simple question as: Is the way I am hearing this, the way that I have come to know God in Christ? Does it fit the picture I have of God that Jesus has revealed to me? If it does the passage is valid and authoritative. If not then I cannot accept its validity or authority.*

In this quote this brother reveals the very problem that following his political views regarding the Palestinians has created. He has to reject as invalid and non-authoritative every passage of the Bible that fails to fit in with his political views of how things ought to be. He justifies this by saying that this is how Jesus would want it to be. To him, and his followers, Scripture is no longer there to correct them in any way. My obvious question is: why don't his followers take some sharp scissors and cut out of the Bible all the passages they think are invalid and non-authoritative? Perhaps they want to end up with slimmed-down Bibles. Perhaps they find their Bibles too weighty in more ways than one. On a serious note they have reduced Bible study to the level of learning from (and obeying) only the bits of the Bible that feel nice. They have reduced biblical interpretation to a purely subjective level. My final question in regard to Rev. Ateek and his followers is: how can they claim to have such a monopoly on how Jesus thinks and reveals God to them? Do they have a special line of communication that we Christian Zionists are lacking?

It is clear from what Rev. Ateek has suggested that all he and his followers do with any verse that appears to support the arguments of Christian Zionists is to dismiss that verse as invalid and non-authoritative. An illustration of Ateek's method of biblical exegesis is referred to by Paul Wilkinson in regard to Isaiah 43:3-4. He writes:

> *Unwilling to submit to any scripture which assigns to the nation of Israel a unique role in the purposes of God, Ateek writes, "How do the Egyptians feel about being a ransom for Israel, or Ethiopians and Nabeans who would be given in exchange for Israel? ... There is a great need to de-Zionise these texts."*

Then Ateek goes on to suggest other texts in need of his touch. They too must be de-Zionised. This method of interpreting biblical texts is called relativism. It is a method of interpreting the Bible adopted by liberal theologians and previously rejected by evangelicals. In their pursuit of an anti-Israel agenda followers of the pro-Palestinian lobby are obviously prepared to label any number of verses as in need of de-Zionising. Undoubtedly, following through their political agenda is now so important to these Christians that they are willing to lay on one side any number of scriptural verses in order to follow this agenda. To me, this is a new and very sad development. However, it is a development which I believe all Christians should be made aware of.

In order to understand the importance of the way in which the pro-Palestinian lobby of evangelical Christians have changed their method of interpreting the Bible, one must define the traditional method of biblical interpretation used by evangelicals. To do this I will be referring to the definitions put forward by Roy Zuck in his book 'Basic Bible Interpretation'. Roy Zuck is a respected evangelical theologian.

The explanation of biblical texts in terms of what they mean is called 'exegesis'. One who seeks to interpret and apply biblical texts to Christian belief and practice is called an 'exegete'. Roy Zuck suggests:

> *We assume that each word in a passage has a normal, literal meaning, unless there is a good reason to view it as a figure of speech. The exegete does not go out of his way to spiritualize or allegorize. Words mean what words mean. So if the Bible mentions a 'horse' it means 'a horse'. When the Bible speaks of the 'Promised Land', it means a literal land given to Israel and should not be interpreted as a reference to Heaven.*

Roy Zuck goes on to explain that Bible scholars should also seek to understand the meaning of any biblical passage in relation to the historical setting in which its author wrote it. This involves considering the geography, the customs, the current events and the political situation that prevailed at the time that a biblical passage was written. Obviously any teacher of biblical truths needs to often make reference to Bible dictionaries, commentaries and books which seek to explain the historical background. Roy Zuck also suggests:

The best interpreter of scripture is scripture itself. We must examine a passage in its immediate context (the verses surrounding it), its wider context (the book in which it is found) and in its complete context (the Bible as a whole). The Bible does not contradict itself. Any theological statement made in one verse can, and should be harmonized with theological statements in other parts of scripture. Good Bible interpretation relates any one passage to the total content of scripture.

By this accepted evangelical method of biblical interpretation the theological assertions of Christian Zionists are seen to be based on a sound biblical exegesis. In order to suggest that Christian Zionists don't base their beliefs on a correct interpretation of biblical passages, the pro-Palestinian lobby have adopted a method of biblical exegesis that is purely subjective, based on how an individual feels that Jesus might have related to either an Old Testament or New Testament passage. This has opened the door for weird and wonderful doctrines to be developed among the adherents of this theological lobby, based purely on how they feel. For example, Barbara Rossing, a member of this theological lobby and regular speaker at Sabeel conferences arranged by Naim Ateek, has reached some rather fanciful conclusions about the Book of Revelation and the role of Jesus as the Lamb of God. Paul Wilkinson refers to these very peculiar beliefs in the following manner:

Rossing believes that the Book of Revelation presents a vision, not of judgment and destruction, but of renewal and healing, all of which is made possible through 'Lamb power'. In outlining her 'Lamb theology', Rossing depicts the Lord Jesus as 'lambkin', 'lamby' and even 'fluffy'.

I would suggest that the subjective, feeling-based exegesis developed by the pro-Palestinian lobby runs contrary to the advice that Apostle Paul gave to his disciple Timothy in the New Testament. In 2 Timothy 2:15 Paul instructs Timothy to study well and to correctly handle the scriptures as the word of truth. Since the New Testament was only just in the process of being written Paul was obviously referring to the Old Testament as the Word of Truth. In the light of this, I ask, how would any of us think that the authors of the Old Testament were inspired to only write some of it and not all of it? How dare we suggest that prophets like Isaiah and Jeremiah were inspired by xenophobia in some of their writings yet at other times were inspired by the Holy Spirit to predict accurately the Messianic passages that Jesus so wonderfully fulfilled?

I do not think that Jesus would want us to de-Zionise parts of the Bible. He identified himself so clearly with his Jewish people when he told the Samaritan woman that he met at Jacob's Well that the Samaritans worshipped the one that they did not know but he, as a Jew, worshipped the one that they did know. He then said, conclusively, that salvation is of the Jews, or as some versions translate it 'is *from* the Jews' (see John 4:22). According to Mark's Gospel, Jesus answered the Sadducees' question about the widow that married seven brothers by stating clearly that he believed that God was, and will always be, the God of Abraham, Isaac and Jacob. In stating this he was quoting from Exodus 3:15, the words spoken to Moses by God himself. Jesus' reference to this fact implies very clearly that he believed in God's unchanging nature. It also implies that he believed that God has established an unchanging covenant with the descendants of these Patriarchs, namely the Jewish people (see Mark 12:18-27).

The apostle Paul stated that he also believed that God would always have a special relationship with the Jewish people on account of his promises to Abraham, Isaac and Jacob (see Romans 11:26-29). At no point did Jesus ever refer to himself as a Palestinian. No other Jewish writer living at the time of Jesus ever referred to themselves as a Palestinian. Even Pilate, the Roman governor, wrote above Jesus' cross, "Jesus King of the Jews," not "King of Palestine". Jesus was called "Jesus of Nazareth" during his lifetime, but never "Jesus the Palestinian". His disciples were referred to as Galileans in the New Testament, but never Palestinians.

In my opinion, the pro-Palestinian lobby are guilty of re-creating the historical Jesus to fit in with their political view of what they think he should be. Their Christ of Faith is radically different from the real historical Jesus. Some of the pro-Palestinian lobby seem willing to identify with any Arab dictator, any Arab extremist, as long as it might forward the political cause of the Palestinian people. They seem to believe that only the State of Israel has committed acts of inhumanity in the Middle East.

I do not condone serious errors made by governments that have ruled Israel. Sadly all human governments are prone to make such serious errors, especially during times when they are at war. The British government was itself responsible for some terrible acts of barbarity against innocent German civilians when our air-force bombed Nazi cities indiscriminately. Such terror attacks were motivated by a desire for revenge rather than to shorten the duration of the war. Strategic bombing of industrial and military sites would have had the impact of shortening the war. Sadly the desire for revenge took over and the consequence was that thousands upon thousands of civilians were brutally murdered.

The pro-Palestinian lobby seem most reluctant to stand up for the freedom of Arabs beyond the Palestinian cause that they espouse. They do not seem to speak out against the thousands of Arab civilians murdered by President Assad in Syria. At the same time this lobby fails to give the government of Israel any praise for their willingness to offer free medical treatment to the Palestinian casualties that came as a result of the dreadful fighting that took place when Hamas and Fatah supporters fought over which faction should be dominant in the territory ruled by the Palestinian Authority. The willingness of the Israelis to offer free medical treatment to their future potential enemies, in my estimation, shows the Israelis in an extremely positive light.

The relative lack of corruption among Israeli politicians, when compared with the terrible corruption of Palestinian politicians, to a great extent explains the poverty of the Palestinian people. Had the Palestinian Authority spent the vast quantity of the aid money that they have received on development and sought a genuine peace with Israel, the Palestinians would have enjoyed a much improved level of prosperity in the territories that they control. The government of Israel would then have eagerly worked with the Palestinian leaders to improve the economic welfare of Jew and Arab alike. I want to see a genuine peace emerge between Israel and the Palestinians. However, I believe it can only be based upon a negotiated settlement that leaves Israel with secure, defensible borders, and the Palestinians with a genuine democracy. It can only take place if Israel's Arab neighbours turn away from their policy of seeking to destroy the State of Israel by military means and formally recognise that Israel has the right to exist. I doubt the willingness of the Arab dictators to seek such a peace. I believe that only the second coming of Jesus himself will bring genuine peace to the whole world. I have never prayed for wars to break out. I have often prayed for both wars and tyranny to end.

The Restoration of the State of Israel: Fulfilment of Biblical Prophecy or Quirk of History?

Advocates of Replacement Theology inevitably have to answer this question by claiming that this great event, which occurred against all the odds in 1948, was simply an unexpected quirk of history. This is the only logical conclusion they can reach since they believe God has rejected the Jews and the nation of Israel from his purposes. This assumption of God's rejection of the Jews means that they have interpreted biblical prophecy regarding the restoration of the Jews to the land God gave to their ancestors as being fulfilled prior to the coming of Jesus or as having some spiritual, non-literal fulfilment relating to the Church.

Christian Zionists believe that the restoration of the State of Israel was indeed a fulfilment of biblical prophecy. Thus we consider that it has a vital significance that all Christian believers should be made aware of. We believe that the attitude our national leaders take in regard to their relationship toward the State of Israel will bring either God's blessing or judgment upon our nations.

In order to understand the prophecies of the Old Testament in regard to the restoration of the Jewish people back to the land of Israel it is important that one recognises that the Jewish people have twice been exiled from their land and have re-gathered there. Their first exile happened in two parts. First the northern kingdom, called Israel, suffered military defeat at the hands of the Assyrians. Their defeat resulted in most of the people from the northern kingdom being taken as exiles to Assyria. Then the Assyrian empire was defeated by the Babylonian empire. Secondly the southern kingdom of Judah was defeated by the Babylonians and all their prominent citizens were taken to exile in Babylon. This process of exiling the Jewish people from their land was completed in 586 BC when Solomon's temple and the walls of Jerusalem were destroyed. The biblical prophets consistently pointed out that the events, which culminated in the exile of the Jews, happened because of the terrible sins of both rulers and citizens of both the northern kingdom of Israel and the southern kingdom of Judah. God had explicitly warned the Jewish people that their sin would result in their exile from the land he gave them in Deuteronomy 29:22-28. He had sent numerous prophets to warn them of the terrible consequences of their sins if they failed to repent. Despite these warnings repentance never occurred, and death, destruction and exile were the result. However, this was not the end of the story. After years of exile, at the order of Cyrus, the King of Persia, who had forcibly taken over the empire of the Babylonians, the Jews were allowed to return to their land. There is no doubt that the biblical prophets rightly predicted this wonderful event.

Sadly, the Jewish people were to experience both the destruction of the new Temple (Herod's Temple) in Jerusalem once again in AD 70 and yet another exile from their land. These events were clearly prophesied by Jesus in Matthew chapter 24, Mark chapter 13 and Luke chapter 21. To some extent this exile was effectively ended in 1948 when the State of Israel came into being. All Jews now have the right of return to the Jewish State. Many have chosen, as yet, not to exercise this right. More Jews currently live in voluntary exile from the land of Israel in the nations where they are settled (especially the U.S.A.) than in Israel. All of these basic historical facts we would agree on. It has been necessary to outline this history of the Jewish people so that my analysis of the difference of biblical interpretation between these different schools of thought can be properly understood.

Proponents of Replacement Theology believe that biblical prophecy only predicts the first restoration of the Jewish people to their land after the Assyrian-Babylonian exile. They believe that God was responsible for ending this exile and restoring the Jews back to their land once more. They believe that after the death and resurrection of Jesus, God effectively ended all interest in the Jews as a distinct racial group. They ceased to be in any sense God's chosen people. Thus, the Bible never prophesied the second restoration of the Jews back to their land, according to them. In effect they believe that God had nothing at all to do with the rebirth of the State of Israel in 1948. They believe that God has nothing to do with the preservation of the State of Israel in modern times. In practice most proponents of Replacement Theology are more sympathetic to the

Palestinians than they are to the Jews. Christian Zionists believe that
biblical prophecy not only predicts this first restoration but it predicts a
second restoration of the Jews to their land following their exile in AD 70.
They also believe that God has brought about this second restoration and
has effectively preserved the State of Israel since its rebirth in 1948.

The question of who is right in our interpretation of the Bible
regarding Israel's restoration to their land is of vital significance. Both
groups cannot be right in their interpretation of biblical prophecy. One
group or the other must be guilty of seriously misunderstanding the plans
and purposes of God regarding the Jewish people today and the State of
Israel. The only way to determine which group is right and which is wrong
is to carefully examine biblical prophecy itself.

One of the most interesting prophecies of the Jewish people being
restored to their own land is found in Isaiah 49:8-26. This prophecy has
some amazing aspects to it that can only be properly applied to the
restoration of the Jews to their own land which has taken place since the
recreation of the State of Israel in 1948. In verse 19 God explains, through
the words of his prophet, that the land that is restored to them is too
narrow for the returning exiles. This same view is reinforced again in the
next verse. When Cyrus allowed the Jews to return to their land from their
first exile, having room to settle in was not an issue. So many Jews had
died in the wars that led up to their first exile that having too many
returning exiles to settle in the land was simply not the case.

These verses only make any sense when applied to the returning
exiles following the restoration of the State of Israel which has occurred in
1948. Now the land of Israel seems far too small for all the Jewish exiles
to return to, if they all claimed their right of return. Even more specifically
the land is too narrow. From east to west the Jewish State is an extremely
narrow strip of land, especially since much of the West Bank has been
given back to the Arabs as a result of the Israeli-Palestinian Peace
Accords. At its narrowest point the territory of Israel extends only 15 km
or 9 miles from east to west. To me the prophecy that God gave through
the prophet Isaiah is remarkably accurate down to the last detail when
applied to the Jewish exiles returning to the modern State of Israel.

Another remarkable point is made in this passage in verse 22. Here Isaiah predicts that the Gentiles will become very closely involved in the restoration of the Jewish exiles to their land, even to the extent of carrying Jewish children on their shoulders. Although King Cyrus, a Gentile, was involved very much in opening the way for the Jews to be returned to their land following their first exile, no other Gentiles were markedly involved in the process. Certainly no Gentiles were seen to be carrying Jewish children on their shoulders. This verse has only been fulfilled in the restoration of the exiles to their land after 1948.

My friend, the late Phil Hunter and his dear wife Norma, have been two Gentiles wonderfully involved in fulfilling this prophecy as they served the returning exiles during the ministry of Exobus. From tiny beginnings they helped thousands of Jewish people to return to their homeland from the new republics that made up the former Soviet Union. Only through Christian Gentiles could this prophecy realistically be fulfilled. No other group of Gentiles have ever helped the Jewish people in such ways. The 'signal' or 'banner' to the nations is obviously Jesus, the Messiah of Israel. He has made it possible for Jew and Gentile to work so closely together. I still await the fulfilment of verse 23, but I am confident that this aspect of the prophecy of Isaiah will one day be clearly fulfilled. I don't think any proponent of Replacement Theology could explain how verse 22 was in any sense fulfilled in the events of the first restoration of the Jews back to their land. This clearly must be a reference to the restoration of the Jews to their land after 1948.

Another important prophecy regarding the restoration of the Jews to their land was made by the prophet Jeremiah in chapter 31. The first important point to make about this chapter is that Jeremiah prophesied that God would establish his new covenant with the House of Israel and the House of Judah. This specific prophecy makes it rather difficult to spiritualise the passage and apply it to the Gentile Church. At the time Jeremiah gave this prophecy, the Jews had been divided into the Kingdom of Israel and the Kingdom of Judah. This division had been acrimonious, and the kingdoms had even reached the point of fighting each other on occasions. The northern kingdom, Israel, had been defeated by the Assyrians, and its leading citizens had been exiled. The Jewish religious and political leaders of the southern kingdom, Judah, remained confident concerning the survival of their kingdom. They believed God would not allow them to be defeated or their Temple, built by King Solomon, to be destroyed.

Against the backdrop of severe opposition from these leaders, Jeremiah and other faithful prophets predicted the defeat of Judah, the exile of its leading citizens and the destruction of the Temple. They were fully vindicated as things happened fully in line with their prophecies. In chapter 31:31 Jeremiah made the remarkable prediction that this division between the north of Israel and the south would end and that God's new covenant would be established with representatives of the citizens of the north and south. This was fulfilled perfectly when Jesus had his Last Supper with his disciples drawn from both sides of this divide and set up the communion as the central rite of the new covenant which he was establishing by the shedding of his blood (see Luke 22:20).

It is abundantly clear from the words of Jeremiah 31:31 and the fulfilment of these words in Jesus' last supper that the new covenant was established not with the Gentile Church, as many Christians seem to think, but with the Jews. This makes the claim that God replaced the Jews as his chosen people by choosing the Gentile Church look ridiculous. How can the claims of Replacement Theology be true when it is clear that the new covenant was established with the Jews? It seems obvious to me that the wonderful promises of God found in verses 35 to 37 are linked to the establishment of the new covenant with the House of Israel and the House of Judah. In these verses God promised that as long as the ordinances of creation exist so will the nation of Israel continue to exist as a nation before him. In the same way God's promise that Jerusalem will be wonderfully rebuilt, contained in verse 38, seems to be clearly linked to the establishment of the new covenant. This being the case, it is then logical to conclude that the rebuilding of Jerusalem is due entirely to the providence of God himself. This suggests that God has been positively involved in the re-gathering of the Jews back to their land.

In chapter 32 Jeremiah prophesies with very much the same theme - of Israel's physical restoration to their land and their spiritual restoration.

He implies that the spiritual restoration flows out of their natural return to the land that God gave to them.

In this chapter some astounding predictions are made which do not fit in with the theory that God is speaking of the restoration of the Jews to their land following their Babylonian exile. When the Jews returned from the Babylonian and Assyrian exile they came only from the lands of the north. Yet in verse 37 of this chapter God promises to bring them out of all the countries where he had driven them. This could only apply to what has happened during the twentieth and twenty-first centuries. In verse 40 of this chapter God clearly indicates that he is making an everlasting covenant with the returning exiles. I ask the important question here: what does an 'everlasting covenant' mean? To me the answer is obvious. It means God is establishing an agreement with these returning exiles which will never come to an end. This is entirely opposite to the beliefs of the advocates of Replacement Theology. They believe that God has forsaken his covenant with the Jews and their present re-gathering to the land of Israel is not at all his design.

Logically the issue of the spiritual restoration of the Jews now needs to be addressed. I see signs of this spiritual restoration already taking place. No one can deny the fact that the growth of the Messianic community among the Jews living in Israel and across the nations has been spectacular. The fact that so much of Jewish society has become secularised does not mean that God cannot bring about such a spiritual revival among the Jewish people. Times were extremely dark in England prior to the Wesleyan revival. Yet within a few decades such an incredible spiritual revival occurred that its impact markedly transformed English society. Some historians have even suggested that the Wesleyan revival in England prevented England going through a violent revolution like that which occurred in France. I believe that the Jews being restored back to their land will lead to the spiritual revival that Jeremiah predicted with such clarity. I believe that this is the spiritual revival that the apostle Paul predicted in Romans 11:25-27. As we shall see, this spiritual revival flowing from the restoration of the Jews to the land of Israel was also prophesied by the prophet Ezekiel. The concept was also developed in the writings of the prophet Zechariah.

The Restoration of the State of Israel: Fulfilment of Biblical Prophecy or Quirk of History?

One of the most notable prophecies regarding the restoration of the Jews to the land of Israel is found in Ezekiel chapter 37:11. Although the bones coming together can be used as an illustration of people coming together in Christ, it should be pointed out that this is not the main theme of this prophecy. It is solely about the restoration of the Jewish people to the land of Israel followed by their spiritual restoration to serve the God of Israel. Any other illustrations it provides are secondary to its main purpose.

Sadly, in the Pentecostal tradition in which I grew up, I heard many sermons based on this chapter which completely ignored the central purpose. We evangelical Christians are quick to point out the way the so-called Jehovah's Witnesses take biblical passages out of context to justify their unscriptural teachings. Is it not equally wrong for ministers of the gospel to preach sermons on biblical passages without acknowledging the primary purpose behind the passage they are expounding?

It is interesting to note that Ezekiel sets out how the peoples of the northern kingdom and the southern kingdom will be united under the reign of the Messiah in verses 19 to 24. This of course took place at the new covenant meal Jesus had with his disciples on the night he was betrayed, but will be completely fulfilled when Jesus returns at his second coming. Thus we can see the different prophets of the Old Testament are united in proclaiming these important themes regarding the events that they were accurately foretelling.

In verse 25 of this chapter Ezekiel points out that the restoration of the Jews to the land of Israel which he is foretelling in this particular prophecy will be of a permanent duration. He states clearly that the descendants of those who return to their land will 'dwell there forever'. In fact they are still in possession of their land when the Messiah returns to govern the whole earth. This leaves the Bible scholar who seeks to interpret this passage with only two conclusions that can be made regarding it. They can either admit that Ezekiel was foretelling accurately the re-gathering of the Jews back to their land in the twentieth and twenty first centuries or suggest that if he was foretelling their return from the Babylonian-Assyrian exile he got his prophecy badly wrong.

The descendants of those Jews that returned from the Babylonian-Assyrian exile did not remain in control of the land of Israel. They were forcibly scattered again in AD 70 by the emperor of Rome and his legions of soldiers. This leaves the advocates of Replacement Theology, who on the whole would claim to be evangelical in their theology, with a dilemma. Either they admit that Ezekiel misheard God's word in regard to this issue and thus deny the divine inspiration of Scripture, which they profess to hold as a central theological belief, or they admit that the Prophet Ezekiel correctly foretold the re-gathering of the Jews to the land of Israel in the twentieth and twenty-first centuries. Obviously if one accepts that Ezekiel correctly prophesied this re-gathering by divine guidance then one can only conclude that God has played a major role in the re-establishment of the State of Israel in 1948. Christian Zionists await with joy the fulfilment of the spiritual restoration of the Jewish people which Ezekiel foretold in chapter 37 of his book. My great desire is to still be alive and serving the God of Israel when this spiritual restoration takes place. This spiritual revival will be like 'life from the dead' according to the prophetic word given by Apostle Paul in Romans 11:15.

Another important passage that relates to the Jewish people being re-gathered from exile to the land of Israel is found in Isaiah 43:4-6. In these verses the prophet Isaiah indicates that the Jews will be re-gathered to the land of Israel from north, south, east and west. He goes on to tell that this re-gathering of the Jews will take place even from the ends of the earth. This prediction regarding the extent of the re-gathering does not fit with the historical facts related to the end of the Babylonian and Assyrian exile. It fits far better with the re-gathering of the Jews which has taken place during the twentieth and twenty first centuries. This is yet more strong biblical evidence that the re-gathering of the Jews related to the rebirth of the State of Israel in 1948 was clearly predicted by the Old Testament prophets.

Thus the evidence suggests that God has been very much involved in the rebirth of the State of Israel and the re-gathering of the Jews back to their land. This surely indicates that the advocates of Replacement Theology are wrong in their assertion that God has abandoned the Jews and replaced them in his plans by choosing the Gentile Church instead of them.

It is difficult to maintain the view that Isaiah 43 relates only to their restoration following their Babylonian-Assyrian exile. Following this exile they only returned to Israel from the north (Assyria and Babylon) and from the south (the Jews which had escaped to the lands of North Africa). They certainly did not return to the land of Israel from 'the ends of the earth' as Isaiah indicated. His words could only be accurately applied to the return of the Jews to the State of Israel.

No doubt all these prophets were amazed at the things the Holy Spirit placed upon their hearts to write down and could not conceive of how their words would be fulfilled. Their role in the expounding of God's foreknowledge to the Jews and to the whole of mankind is explained in 2 Peter 1:21. These men obediently wrote down the things the Holy Spirit revealed to them without understanding fully the things that they wrote. The accuracy of these prophecies in regard to future events that these prophets had no influence upon is a wonderful proof of the divine inspiration of the Bible.

Let me explain at this point that I am not implying that I believe that God preordained events to happen by manipulating human free will. I believe that God always respects human free will. Rather I believe that God revealed the things that he knew would take place centuries later through his prophets so that we would know that he is working to shape history through his miraculous intervention in circumstances to defend the rights of the oppressed and fulfil his promises to Abraham, Isaac and Jacob. I believe God always intervenes miraculously through circumstances or willing servants to preserve the Jewish people who are the Sons of Jacob. This is what God indicated through the prophet Malachi in Malachi 3:6. In the same manner Satan and his demon host are always seeking to stir up anti-Jewishness and an insane hatred of Jews in order to frustrate the revealed will of God and destroy God's plan to offer spiritual life to all people through the Jewish people that he has always used to fulfil this wonderful purpose. I believe that Replacement Theology is one of the most serious of wicked acts of deception that the Prince of Darkness has ever designed to frustrate the purposes of God. Unlike God,

Satan is only too willing to manipulate human minds to fulfil his wicked purposes as in the attitudes of the Gentiles that took over the running of the Christian church.

Another interesting reference to the scattering of the Jews among the Gentile nations is made by Jesus in Luke 22:24. In this verse Jesus not only predicts the dispersal of the Jews among all nations which was to occur in AD 70, he also specifically states that at a set time in the future Jerusalem will no longer be "trodden down by the Gentiles". This will occur when the times of the Gentiles are fulfilled or completed. There has been some debate among Bible scholars as to what Jesus meant by these phrases.

To me the first part of what Jesus was referring to is easy to understand. After the brief war of 1967 Jerusalem was re-united under the control of the State of Israel. At this point it ceased being trodden under foot by the Gentiles. In other words it returned to the people God had promised this city to. To me the phrase "trodden under foot" means dominated and controlled by Gentile rulers. In this regard Jesus is undoubtedly predicting events two thousand years into the future. He is, in effect, predicting the re-establishment of the State of Israel. For Jerusalem to no longer be trodden under foot by Gentiles it had to come again under Jewish governance.

However, I must admit that I am not 100% sure of what Jesus meant when he referred to the time of the Gentiles coming to an end. Some commentators have suggested that he might have meant that the Gentile domination of the Church was coming to an end. I have much sympathy with this view. Certainly many thousands of Jews have come to embrace Jesus as their Messiah since 1967. The world 'Messianic Movement' has been birthed and expanded both in Israel and around the world. 'Jews for Jesus' has done much to bring Jews to know their Messiah across Jewish communities world-wide. Other commentators have suggested that Jesus meant God has transferred his attention from an emphasis of working through believing Gentiles to opening the eyes of his Jewish people to recognise Jesus as Messiah. Some have even suggested that now the Gentile times have ended God has taken a controlling interest in world affairs. Now the great Gentile nations only think that they control world events; God, in fact, has taken control of the circumstances affecting all the nations of the world. He is, they claim, punishing the nations for how they are treating the nation of Israel today. This fits well with the prophecy of the Prophet Zechariah (see Zechariah 12:1-3). I believe that God is punishing the national leaders that are trying to get Israel to give up their control of Jerusalem through allowing natural disasters to afflict their nations and through the terrible economic crisis facing the nations of the world.

Sadly much of the Christian church remains unaware of what is taking place. Few, if any, prominent church leaders have sought to warn the world's political leaders of the consequences of their biased policies against the State of Israel. Far too many church leaders have been influenced by Replacement Theology to take seriously the warning contained in these verses. They would rather spiritualise this warning away, claiming that these verses should not be interpreted in any literal sense.

It is interesting to note that the prophet Zechariah also predicts a spiritual revival in the land of Israel that has certainly not taken place as yet. He does this in Zechariah 12:10-13:2. Surely this is the wonderful revival predicted by the other Old Testament prophets and by Apostle Paul in Romans chapter 11.

By now it will be obvious to you that I personally believe that the re-establishment of the State of Israel was no quirk of history but was the fulfilment of biblical prophecy. I believe that God has worked through circumstances to fulfil his promise to the patriarchs - Abraham, Isaac and Jacob - that their descendants are given the land of Israel as part of an everlasting covenant. I also believe that the prophecies regarding a great spiritual revival among the Jews will be wonderfully fulfilled. It is clear to me that all this biblical prophecy that has been fulfilled, and will yet be fulfilled, is a serious wake up call. I recognise that many Christians have accepted this false teaching because it has been taught by Bible teachers they have respected. I urge these brethren to ask God to reveal his truth regarding this vital issue to their hearts as they carefully read through the many scriptural references I have quoted.

Is there Death in the Pot?

Before I draw this chapter to a conclusion it is important for us to consider why the existence of the land of Israel is so vitally important to the Jewish people. The people have a great feeling of insecurity based upon centuries of social exclusion and bitter persecution. Dr. Howard Morgan, himself a Messianic Jew, explained to us Gentile Christians the vital significance of the State of Israel in his book 'For Zion's Sake'. He wrote (p.98):

> *Israel provides a homeland and assures the survival of the Jewish people. Prior to the establishment of the State of Israel, expulsion was an anti-Semitic tactic clearly based on the condition or status of the Jews as permanent aliens. Jews found themselves as a homeless people whose residence was always by permission or privilege. With the establishment of the State of Israel the Jews now have a haven from persecution and a homeland by right rather than by permission.*

We as Gentile believers in Jesus can thus appreciate how centuries of social exclusion and bitter persecution have shaped the Jewish psyche. We can begin to appreciate how important the State of Israel's guarantee of the right of return to all Jews scattered among the nations is to these exiles. Jews have every right to feel threatened by the growing wave of anti-Jewishness sweeping through the nations of the western world. We Christians, being conscious of the debt we all owe to the first Jewish followers of Jesus who risked their lives to spread the gospel to our ancestors, should be the first to stand up and oppose this. In order to do this effectively we need to make ourselves knowledgeable regarding the the history of the State of Israel and the issue of the Palestinians from a factual rather than a biased, partisan perspective too often fostered by our misinformed news media. Sympathetic phone calls from Christians to the embassy staff at the Israeli Embassy are very well received when the State of Israel is unfairly represented in the news. I can testify concerning this from personal experience. Sympathetic Christians can also have a positive impact through contacting our parliamentary representatives when we discern that the State of Israel is being unfairly treated by our media and by our political leaders. The more of us that get involved in campaigning in this manner, the greater our impact will be.

Let us look at it another way. The Socialist Workers Party has an impact far exceeding the number of its active supporters due to the outspoken nature of their membership and their considerable fervour in campaigning for their causes. Should we not become far more vocal in campaigning for truth and fairness to triumph in our societies? Far too often we have remained silent when we should have spoken out for those who are being oppressed and treated unjustly. Perhaps we all need to take on board the words found in the letter of James 4:17. Here we are warned that if we know about the good we should do, yet fail to do it, we are then guilty of sin. I have become increasingly aware of the importance of recognising how many times I have been guilty of committing sins of omission as well as sins of commission. If we recognise how often we have failed our Lord Jesus through sins of omission it will then spur us on to ask for his strength to do the right thing even if we are fearful or reluctant to do the right thing.

Having said all these positive things regarding the re-establishment of the State of Israel, I feel that I must reiterate my sincerely held belief that God loves the Arab peoples too. At our Prayer for Israel meetings, which I lead, we pray positively for Jews and Arabs alike. We pray for both to find a genuine peace in Jesus. What the world media fail to report is the fact that many Arabs have embraced citizenship in the State of Israel and get on really well with the Jews. They also fail to report the fact that many Arab and Jewish believers in Jesus choose to fellowship together in the same church fellowships. The world media fail to stress the fact that Israel is the only democracy in the Middle East - with a free press, free elections (in which Jew and Arab citizens vote together) and a free and impartial judiciary. The terrible oppression that exists in the neighbouring Arab nations at last came to world attention in 2011. Prior to the Spring Uprising in these Arab nations, scant attention was paid to these oppressive regimes by much of the world media. However, the world's media seems to have an obsession with the Israeli-Palestinian issue.

When Israel is attacked, it seems that little attention is given to these attacks by violent terrorists. When Israel defends its citizens there is usually a media outcry regarding its actions. This seems far from balanced reporting. At no point do I wish to defend acts of brutality on either side of this conflict. I would never say that the Israeli government is perfect by any means. But on the other hand neither is any other government in the world.

My final point in this chapter is a true saying I have often quoted to the congregation which I am privileged to lead. This saying is true when one sits down and reviews the facts of Middle Eastern politics and helps to focus one's mind on the reality of the situation. If the State of Israel gave the order for their soldiers to lay down their arms in a unilateral act of disarmament then within hours most of the Jewish citizens of Israel, if not all, would be massacred by their enemies. If on the other hand the enemies of Israel put down their arms there would be peace.

One last thought: the Israelis never took the West Bank or Gaza from any Palestinian government. No such government has ever existed. They took this land from Jordan and Egypt. These Arab countries had previously never recognised 'Palestinians' as being anything other than the Arab citizens of their countries. The Israelis took control of this territory whilst fighting for their right to exist as a nation. Even now the vast countries of Jordan and Egypt are big enough to give the Palestinians a home if only they were willing to do so.

A History of Christian Zionism

Before examining the history of Christian Zionism it is important to define what is meant by the term. The *Zionism and Israel Encyclopaedic Dictionary* offers a definition of this term as "...support for Israel and Zionism among Christians" and "support for the restoration of the Jews based on Christian religious doctrine". The authors of this comprehensive dictionary warn against accepting the stereotypes offered by the proponents of Replacement Theology regarding this term. They suggest that all Christian Zionists are fundamentalist Christians and want Israel to conquer lands way beyond her present borders. In contrast to the stereotypes of Zionist Christians put forward by anti-Zionist Christians like Stephen Sizer, the authors of the *Zionism and Encyclopaedic Dictionary* suggest:

> *The vast majority of Christians who support Zionism and Israel are not fundamentalist... Christian supporters of Israel include and have included Congregationalists, Presbyterians and Roman Catholics such as the Sisters of Zion.*

Sometimes Christians that have a love and appreciation towards the Jewish people can feel rather isolated and marginalised by their fellow believers. Thankfully, this is not our experience. However, I do feel the hurt and confusion many of my fellow believers feel when they endeavour to speak out in defence of the Jewish people; they face censure and rejection. I too have felt the chill of rejection in many different situations when I have tried to speak up in appreciation and defence of the Jewish people.

In response to the opposition Christian Zionists often face among misguided fellow believers, it is encouraging to review the history of Christian Zionism and note that many prominent Christian leaders have viewed biblical prophecy and concluded that God would restore the Jewish people back to their own land and re-gather the exiles from among the nations. Many of them reached this conclusion even when there seemed no feasible way in which the land of Israel could be restored to the

Jews according to their natural perspective. They believed in the restoration of the Jews to their land because they believed that God himself would facilitate the fulfilment of these biblical prophecies.

Given the influence of the doctrine of Replacement Theology upon the Church Fathers it is not surprising that the belief in the restoration of the Jews back to the land of Israel died out among Church leaders. This belief came to prominence again among the second generation of Protestant reformers, especially among the Puritans.

John Owen, the greatest of the Puritan theologians lived from 1616 to 1683. At that time there was no glimmer of hope, no possibility, of the Jews returning to their land. But John Owen believed the Scriptures. He wrote: 'The Jews shall be gathered from all parts of the earth where they are scattered, and brought home into their homeland.'[13]

Another prominent Puritan theologian, Samuel Rutherford, wrote with great excitement and joy of the Jewish people being restored wonderfully to know Jesus as their Messiah.

O see the sight, next to Christ's coming in the clouds, the most joyful. Our elder brethren the Jews and Christ fall upon each other's neck and kiss each other. They have been long asunder; they will be kind to each other when they meet.[14]

Obviously he believed that the words of Apostle Paul in Romans chapter 11 would be fulfilled literally.

Thomas Ice, in his article 'Lovers of Zion', indicates that during the 1660s a whole flurry of books were written by Puritans which argued that it was prophesied clearly throughout the Old Testament that the Jews would one day be re-gathered from among the nations and restored to the land of Israel. These authors argued that Christians should pray for these events to unfold and rejoice when God fulfilled his purposes regarding the Jewish people. The teaching was embraced by a number of Anglican evangelicals throughout the eighteenth and nineteenth centuries. It was

---

[13] *Our Hands are Stained with Blood,* Michael Brown
[14] ibid

also embraced by many evangelicals in the U.S.A. at the end of the eighteenth and during the nineteenth century. President John Quincy Adams stated that he greatly desired to see the Jews settled once again in the land of Palestine. Thomas Ice suggests:

> *From the earliest times, American Christianity has always tilted toward support of the restoration of national Israel in the Holy Land. American Christians, when compared with predominantly anti-Semitic Euro-Asian Christianity, has always had a pro-Semitic disposition. Thus, it is not surprising that this pro-Semitic tradition continues in America today.*

Two of the most influential Christian leaders in the history of the English Church were John and Charles Wesley. It is most worthy of note that both of these great saints believed that God would re-gather the Jewish people and restore them to the land that he had promised them. This is shown in the wonderful hymn composed by Charles Wesley in 1762 entitled 'Almighty God of Love'. John Wesley obviously agreed with the theological content of this hymn because he selected it for his 'Collection of Hymns for the use of the people called Methodists', published in 1780. Herbert Mc Gonigle, in his article 'A Wesley Zionist Hymn', suggests:

> *Its significance lies in the way Charles Wesley looks forward to a restoration of Israel, and how from his re-gathered people, the gospel will spread to all the nations.*

To illustrate the wonderful theological truths this hymn contains I will quote just the fourth and fifth verses.

> *We know it must be done, for God hath spoke the word.*
> *All Israel shall their Saviour own, to their first state restored.*
> *Rebuilt by his command, Jerusalem shall rise,*
> *Her Temple on Moriah stand, again and touch the skies.*

Send then thy servants forth, to call the Hebrews home.
From west and east, and south and north, let all wanderers
Come home.
Where'er in lands unknown, thy fugitives remain,
Bid every creature help them on, thy holy mount to gain.

From reading the lyrics of this hymn it is impossible to conclude that Charles Wesley was not actually referring to the physical restoration of the scattered Jewish exiles to the land of Israel. Remarkably, this hymn goes beyond the physical restoration of the Jewish people to their land. The lyrics of the hymn suggest that their physical restoration back to their land is a necessary preliminary to their spiritual restoration to embrace Jesus as their Messiah. The text of this hymn was reproduced in the Wesleyan 1877 edition of Methodist hymns. In 1983 the words of this hymn were omitted by the committee which established the new Methodist hymn book to be used in the United Kingdom.

No doubt the decision to leave out this great hymn arose from a shift of theological opinion among leading Methodists. Any hint of Christian Zionism had to be removed from the hymn book. Thus, a whole generation of Methodists have grown up without any knowledge of the theological beliefs of their founders in regard to the Jewish people. The question may arise at this point as to why the Wesley brothers did not write more regarding this issue? My answer to this is a simple one. The restoration of the Jews to their land seemed a very long way off to the Wesleys. At that time they were occupied greatly with evangelism and the consequent spiritual revival which arose from this evangelism. Nevertheless, it is undeniable that the Wesley brothers were Zionist in regard to their views regarding the Jewish people. They came to such views by carefully studying the biblical prophecies.

William Hechler, one of the most influential advocates of Christian Zionism in modern times, wrote a powerful appeal to the Church to relate positively to the Jewish people in 1882. In his pamphlet 'The Restoration of the Jews to Palestine according to Prophecy' he predicted that God would soon work to re-establish the Jews in the land of Israel. He urged Christians to pray positively for this to occur and to assist Jews in campaigning for national leaders to facilitate their return to the land. In

1896 he befriended Theodor Herzl, the founder of modern Zionism. He became one of his closest advisors and supporters. In the U.S.A. William Blackstone worked tirelessly to campaign for his fellow Americans to support the Jewish people in returning to their land and re-establishing the State of Israel.

> *In 1891 Blackstone obtained the signatures of 413 prominent Americans and sent this document to President Benjamin Harrison advocating the resettlement of persecuted Jews in Russia to a new homeland in what was then called Palestine. Blackstone later made a similar appeal to President Woodrow Wilson that influenced his acceptance of the Balfour Declaration of 1917. Today in Israel there is a forest named 'Blackstone Forest' in his honour.[15]*

The American acceptance of the Balfour Declaration, which recognised that the Jewish people have a right to a homeland in what was then called Palestine, had enormous significance. It greatly assisted in Britain being given the mandate to govern the territory of Palestine on condition that both Jew and Arab had a right to settle there. Sadly Britain failed to allow sufficient Jews to settle there as to significantly reduce the impact of Hitler's Holocaust in Europe. The British military actively turned back Jews who wanted to escape the threat of the Nazis when their numbers reached the annual quota which the British authorities had set for Jewish immigration. However, the consensus of the world powers agreed in accepting this declaration that the Jews should have an inherent right to resettle their ancient homeland. Blackstone played his role in ensuring that this took place.

In a similar manner President Harry Truman was influenced by the sound Bible teaching he had received during his youth from teachers who had a love for the Jewish people and who believed the many biblical prophecies regarding the restoration of the State of Israel. In 1948 he personally ensured that the vote of the United States was cast in favour of recognising the State of Israel in the forum of the United Nations.

---

[15] Thomas Ice

President Truman did this despite the fact that the State department recommended to him that the United States should not take this action.

This is surely an encouragement to Christian Zionists to stand strong in our faith and be willing to confront anti-Jewishness wherever we find it. American Christian Zionists have over the years demonstrated that they can have a positive impact upon the corridors of power in their country. I refute entirely the argument that this is a dangerous influence. I believe that Christians should be actively speaking out to oppose the constant stream of lies and misinformation that is put forth by our western media against the State of Israel. It is good to recognise the influence of some Christians within our Conservative Party in the UK who have been active within 'Conservatives for Israel'. I have contacted my M.P. at times when I believe our government has been unfair in our relations with the State of Israel. I have also written letters of concern to both our Prime Minister and the Leader of the Opposition when I believe our nation has behaved in an unfair way in relation to the Jewish people and the State of Israel. I believe that we as Christians should exercise our democratic rights to support a balanced and unbiased approach to the Arab-Israeli conflict on the part of our political leaders. Underpinning this approach should be the acceptance on the part of our national leaders that the State of Israel has a right to protect its citizens and defend itself against Arab aggression. I believe that there should also be a degree of recognition, on the part of our national leaders, that Jerusalem should be recognised as the undivided capital of Israel. In the same manner they need to recognise the fact that Israel giving away land for peace has thus far been a completely fruitless policy. Why should this policy bring peace to Israel in the future?

It is encouraging to note that even during the most terrible times of the Holocaust some Christians were willing to risk their lives to protect the Jewish people from their Nazi persecutors. Some of the efforts of these Christians living in Nazi-occupied Europe have been recognised and acclaimed, such as those of the well-known ten-Boom family. Others have not had their stories told widely but similarly risked their lives and even laid them down for the sake of the Jewish people. Many of the 'righteous Gentiles' have been remembered in the Garden of the Righteous in the grounds of the Holocaust Museum in Israel. Thankfully many of the names of Christians are remembered in this garden.

Other famous missionaries, such as William Carey and Henry Martyn, also had a love for the Jewish people and prayed for their restoration back to their homeland. Many believed that their restoration to their homeland would lead to a wonderful spiritual revival among them that would in turn bring fresh life and revival to the Christian church.

Bishop Handley Moule wrote:

The great event of Israel's return to God in Christ, and his to Israel, will be the signal and the means of a vast rise of spiritual life in the universal church, and of an unexampled ingathering of regenerate souls from the world.

In recent times some prominent Christian leaders have spoken out in support of the State of Israel and the Jewish people. These have included the great evangelist Billy Graham, David Pawson, Dr. Howard Morgan, Lance Lambert and Derek Prince.

In praying for Israel our church has been greatly helped by different inter-denominational groups. These have included Prayer for Israel, Christian Friends of Israel, Jews for Jesus, Bridges for Peace, Third Name Link and 49:22 Trust.

Never in all my time of reading literature from these Christian Zionist groups have I ever read anything overtly anti-Arab or encouraging us to pray for Israel to launch military attacks on her Arab neighbours in order for her to extend her borders. By contrast, if one should read Arab literature studied by children in the Palestinian areas it would be filled with anti-Jewish propaganda, aimed at inciting hatred against all Jewish people. This literature is not only aimed at campaigning for the creation of a Palestinian State with Jerusalem as its capital, it is totally anti-Semitic in tone.

Jewish people, as a whole, are represented as being totally corrupt and evil. I have studied some of this literature found easily on the internet whilst researching articles in preparation for writing this book. The compassionate nature of the Israeli government was demonstrated during the terrible civil war between Hamas and Fatah, the two main Palestinian parties. During this conflict Israel offered to send ambulances into the Palestinian areas to pick up and treat the injured on both sides of the conflict. When this offer was declined by both Hamas and Fatah, Israeli ambulances waited at the crossing points to the Palestinian areas and ferried the Palestinian injured to Jewish hospitals where they received free treatment. Had it not been for this act of compassion on the part of the Israelis the Palestinian medical services would have been completely overwhelmed by this crisis, and many more injured Palestinian fighters would have died. This was a remarkable act of compassion considering that these fighters the Israeli medics were treating might one day be involved in attacks upon the State of Israel and its citizens.

Even Christian Zionists who believe that the borders of Israel will in the future be greatly extended also believe that God himself, and not them, will be the agent through whom this takes place. Most of them do not seek to precipitate these events by their own actions.

Mikael Knighton, in his work 'Christian Zionism Defined', states:

A common rebuttal serving to debunk and discredit the underlying objectives of Christian Zionism is the short-sighted argument purporting that Christian Zionists seek to facilitate the literal fulfilment of Bible prophecy- specifically, the end of the world and the subsequent return of Yeshua (Jesus) the Messiah. Quick to dismiss the biblical significance of Israel as a nation and as a people, as well as the longevity of God's faithful and everlasting covenants with her, opponents of Christian Zionism... do not recognise God's biblical commands for Christians to support the Jewish people.

One of the most prominent modern advocates of Christian Zionism is John Hagee, minister of the Conerstone church in San Antonio, Texas. On his website he states some vital truths that all Christians should be reminded of. He suggests:

Every Christian should remember the debt of gratitude the Christian community owes to the Jewish community. The Jewish people don't need Christianity to explain their existence or their origin. But Christians cannot explain their existence without Judaism. It was Jewish people that gave us the written Scriptures. They gave us the patriarchs, Abraham, Isaac and Jacob. They gave us the disciples and the apostle Paul. The Jewish people gave to Christianity the first Christian family, Mary, Joseph and Jesus, our Saviour. If you take away the Jewish contribution to Christianity, there is nothing left.

He also summarises the truth about the geopolitical reality of the Middle East region in a most succinct manner. The truth of his observation has been greatly vindicated by the shocking, unfolding events of the recent Arab uprisings and the reactions of the Arab dictatorial rulers to these legitimate cries from their peoples for freedom and democracy. He states:

Geopolitically speaking, we should support Israel because it is the only true democracy in the Middle East. The tiny democracy of Israel is surrounded by feudal states and brutal dictatorships that control vast regions of land and oil resources. The presence of the Israeli Defence Forces brings stability to that part of the world.

The omens are not really that encouraging in regard to the establishment of a Palestinian State in the coming months or years. Despite the appearance of a degree of peace emerging between the Palestinian factions of Hamas and Fatah, they still remain bitterly divided. There is the likelihood of a new civil war emerging in the Palestinian territories soon after the establishment of Palestinian statehood. Neither of the two Palestinian factions has a good track record in respecting human rights. Fatah had a dreadful record with respect to economic corruption and nepotism during the rulership of Yasser Arafat. The corruption of the Palestinian Authority, as governed by Fatah, was one of the major reasons that the Palestinians in Gaza elected the extremist government of Hamas to rule the province. Following their election, Hamas proved much better at providing services to their populace without the serious threat of funds being diverted into the bank accounts of corrupt politicians. However, Hamas quickly spoiled things by launching unprovoked missile attacks on Israeli territory, thus forcing Israel to retaliate and seriously damage the infrastructure of Gaza and the economy.

One cannot help feeling sorry for the ordinary Palestinians who have to tolerate so much corruption and ineptitude on the part of their politicians.

Knowing that so many Christians across the ages have shared with Christian Zionists today the same understanding of the biblical prophecies is surely an encouragement to those of us who have this understanding of the Scriptures. The fact that Replacement Theology is so widely believed among so many Christians is no proof that this doctrine is right. I hope that the evidence that I have presented in this book will persuade some brethren that have previously been influenced by this false teaching to reject it. I also pray that God may use the things that I have written to help some of my fellow Christians to consider the implications of this message. In the same way I pray that the things I have written will help some of my fellow believers to be better equipped to argue intelligently and lovingly with fellow brethren who have been misled by the teachings of Replacement Theology.

Psalm 83: A Prophetic Psalm?

Psalm 83 was written about 3000 years ago, during the reign of King David. The author of the psalm was a musician called Asaph. He was also referred to as a seer in 2 Chronicles 29:30. The Hebrew word for 'seer' is 'chozeh'. The meaning of this word is 'one that is gifted with prophetic inclination'. This Hebrew word is often used in relation to the great biblical prophets. When Asaph composed this psalm Israel was in a strong position both militarily and economically in the Middle East region. Israel was not facing any immediate threat of invasion from any of its neighbours. The Philistine threat had ended.

In effect the psalm could not be interpreted as referring to the situation that Israel was in when Asaph composed it. It had to refer to future threats that Israel would face from a confederation of its neighbouring states. I believe that this psalm makes specific references to the Arab states surrounding much of the modern State of Israel and their united action against the Jewish state that cannot be applied to any other time in the history of the Jewish people. Thus, the words of this prophetic song disprove the assertion of the advocates of Replacement Theology that God is no longer involved in fulfilling his ancient covenant with the people of Israel. If this central belief of the advocates of Replacement Theology is seen to be false then the whole doctrine is undermined.

Psalm 83 begins with a prayer that God will not keep silent or fail to intervene concerning the large confederation of states that have made a covenant to destroy the nation of Israel. Many Arabs, including Hamas and Hezbollah and Iran, have made it clear that their aim is not to secure an enduring peace with Israel based upon the granting of statehood to the Palestinians and an agreement to share the land which was once called Palestine. They want an end to the State of Israel existing in any form. In verse 3, Asaph makes it clear that some of the groups which are seeking to wipe out Israel as a nation work with a degree of subtlety and craftiness. Fatah, although claiming to want a peaceful two-state solution to the deadlock with Israel, seems to be rather insincere in its assertion. Schoolchildren in the West Bank under Fatah's control are taught that it is their duty to hate the Jewish people. Their history textbooks are filled with anti-Jewish images and rhetoric. The leaders of Fatah want to receive aid from western governments; therefore they profess to want a peaceful two-state solution to their impasse with Israel. Privately, they have to play down their desire for a peaceful solution so they don't see their political rivals, the extremist Hamas, making political headway in the West Bank at their expense. Losing control in Gaza was indeed a bitter setback for these leaders. They certainly do not want to see this happen in their West Bank stronghold.

I believe that other Arab states in the Middle East, whilst professing their desire for peace with Israel, really want to see an end to the Jewish state. They want to see this objective achieved because this is what the vast majority of their citizens want. Their citizens have been consistently exposed to bitter propaganda which is not only anti-Israeli but extremely anti-Jewish. One example of this is the way the 'Protocols of the Elders of Zion', a fraudulent and bitterly anti-Jewish document, has been circulated among all the Arab nations of the Middle East. Even apparently moderate Arab leaders have failed to stop this bitter anti-Jewish propaganda circulating among their citizens. They have to speak warm words about wanting peace with Israel, on occasions, to please western leaders. However, their real desire has always been an end of the Zionist state. They aim to do this by weakening the Israeli Defence Forces through the surrender of Israeli territory in return for temporary peace. At the right time they hope that a concerted Arab attack will finally destroy the State of Israel.

One reason the Muslim Arab states of the Middle East want an end to the Jewish state is that many Muslims believe that once a territory has become part of the House of Islam it should always remain Islamic. The territory the Israelis now control once belonged to the Muslim Ottoman Empire. To these Muslims it is a great shame that this territory has passed out of Muslim control. They dearly want this territory to again be restored to the House of Islam. Thus, one can see that the content of verse 3 of this psalm seems to so clearly describe the situation in the Middle East today.

Each of the ancient Arab nations mentioned in this psalm correspond to members of the modern alliance of Arab states and the

Palestinians against Israel. The author of the website www.bible411.com explains:

> *Obviously the Philistines represent the Palestinians. Edom, Moab and Ammon occupied what is the modern state of Jordan. Gebal is Lebanon (Joshua 13:5-6). Iraq was populated by the Hagarenes or Hagarites that dwelt east of Gilead in the wilderness of the River Euphrates (1 Chronicles 5:1, 9-10). The Ishmaelites settled in what is now Saudi Arabia and Ishmael's eldest son, Nabajoth, is identified with Syria... Bible scholars and historians agree that ancient Israel was never confronted by such an elaborate alliance of nations... Therefore, this prophecy must have an end time fulfilment.*

It is, at first sight, surprising to find that the Philistines are mentioned as part of this coalition by Asaph since during his lifetime he saw the Philistines completely defeated by Israel during the reign of King David. Only through the inspiration of the Holy Spirit could Asaph make such an amazing claim regarding the Philistines in the psalm that he composed - a claim that would have appeared totally illogical to him. There is no way he could have naturally understood that the word 'Philistine' would evolve into the word 'Palestine'. There is no way he could have understood by natural means that a group of Arabs would later refer to themselves as 'Palestinians'.

Walid Shoebat, in his article 'Psalm 83 and Islam', expresses his belief that this psalm is prophetic and describes the present day Arab-Israeli conflict. Psalm 83:11-12 relates back to the story of how God delivered the Israelites during the time of the great Judge Gideon. Oreb, Zeeb, Zebah and Zalmunna were the great princes of the Midianites who had occupied much of the land of Israel. The account of these events is found in the book of Judges in chapters 7 and 8. The Midianites massively outnumbered any armed force that the Israelites could raise up to fight them. Gideon was then asked to reduce Israel's fighting force down to three hundred men, so that the Israelites would be able to recognise that God alone had brought about their deliverance. These three hundred men surrounded the camp of the Midianites, revealing their hidden torches and blowing their trumpets and shouting at the right moment. The consequence of this was that God struck the Midianites with panic, and they ended up fighting among themselves and fleeing in terror from the Israelites.

Walid Shoebat suggests that this is exactly what happened in modern times during the Six Day War in 1967. He recounts his experience, prior to his conversion to Christianity, when he felt the panic shared by the Arab forces when confronting Israeli forces much smaller than their own. He estimates that the Israeli Defence Forces were outnumbered at least one hundred to one. As a Muslim Arab he was left totally at a loss to explain why the invading Arab forces fled with such fear. He draws the obvious parallel between the events recounted in the Book of Judges, referred to in Psalm 83, and the events that he experienced prior to his conversion, during the Six Day War. He believes that it was only God's intervention that prevented Israel's defeat and the end of the State of Israel. He believes that this psalm accurately prophesied these events. These events left a lasting impression upon him that helped to bring about his conversion.

My dear friend Brother B (whose identity I need to protect due to the existence of death threats against him and his family) commented on exactly the same thing, following his conversion from Islam to Christianity. He too had been left completely bemused by the failure of the Arab armies to destroy the State of Israel in both 1967 and 1973. He was left pondering why, if Allah is truly God, did he allow the failure of these Muslim armies despite their undoubted military superiority in relation to the Israeli forces. After his conversion, he ascribed these Israeli victories solely to the actions of the true God, the God of Israel, in fulfilling the words of this prophetic psalm.

It is most noticeable that during the great battle recounted in the Book of Judges, the Midianite forces ended up fighting each other. I believe that this reference is also prophetic of how Israel's Arab enemies have so often been divided against one another. Divisions within the House of Islam are most apparent. Hardly a day passes without some reference on our news stations concerning the Sunni and Shi'ite branches of Islam launching murderous attacks upon one another. The terrible division between Arab rulers and their citizens has been highlighted in a most dramatic way throughout 2011. The Palestinians are also divided into two antagonistic factions: Fatah and Hamas. Only a few years ago they fought a bitter civil war within the areas governed by the Palestinian Authority. They have signed a peace accord, but underlying tensions still exist between these two factions. The leaders of Fatah are left controlling the West Bank territory, and Hamas are left controlling the Gaza Strip.

I believe that Christians called to pray for the peace of Jerusalem should pray for both Jews and Arabs alike. I pray that Arabs, like Walid Shoebat, find their peace in Jesus. However, for those militants that are intent on fighting Israel, I pray that they will be divided against one another as were the forces of these Arab princes referred to in Psalm 83. I believe that the division within Islam and between Hamas and Fatah are a witness that this prophetic prayer is being fulfilled in a most powerful way.

When I was privileged to be able to visit Israel in 1987, I had the joy of being taken to see some of the sights around Jerusalem by a Christian Arab taxi driver. He rejoiced to be an Israeli citizen and was totally opposed to the highly corrupt leadership of the P.L.O. He discussed with me Psalm 83 and shared with me how reading this psalm and understanding its prophetic fulfilment had helped to bring about his conversion from Islam to Christianity. He shared the same insights that Walid Shoebat has expressed in his article. My experience of meeting both Israeli Jews and Arabs was further proof to me that I was right to hold fast to my interpretation of Scripture. I enjoyed having tea with my new Arab friend and his family. His family all shared with me the joy of being Israeli Arabs.

Walid Shoebat has brought to light an interesting similarity between the Midianites at the time of Gideon and the Muslim Arabs that are set upon the destruction of the State of Israel. He points out the fact that according to Judges 8:21 the ornaments on the necks of the Midianite camels were in the shape of crescent moons. It is interesting to note that the crescent moon is now found on the flags of many of the Arab nations that oppose modern day Israel as well as on the top of mosques. It is surely no mere coincidence that Psalm 83 suggests that the future enemies of Israel will be exactly like the Midianite army that fought Israel at the time of Gideon. The Midianite enemies of ancient Israel held that the crescent moon was sacred to them; so do the Arab enemies of Israel today.

What particularly stands out from the opening verses of this psalm is that the possession of the land of Israel is of vital importance to God. God's enemies express their hatred towards him by endeavouring to take the land from those to whom God had allotted it. I believe that Stephen Sizer is sincerely wrong regarding his contention that God is not interested in the ownership of a piece of real estate in the Middle East. He is interested in the ownership of the land called Israel because he made an everlasting covenant with the Jewish people. Part of this covenant relates to their possession of this land. Asaph makes it abundantly clear at the start of this psalm that the nations that attempt to dispossess the State of Israel of its land are by their actions showing themselves to be the enemies of God.

God's Love: The Only Antidote to the Poison in the Pot

In the introduction to this book I began by suggesting that Replacement Theology is a spiritual poison that has poisoned the life of the Church for nearly two thousand years. I compared the poison of Replacement Theology to the poisonous root that one of the sons of the prophets had inadvertently introduced into the pot of stew that had been provided for both him and his companions. This incident relating to the poison in the pot is found in 2 Kings 4:38-41. Like the poisonous root that poisoned the whole of the contents of the pot, at first sight the doctrine of Replacement Theology seems to be a reasonable teaching that has a certain degree of logic behind it. It does certainly seem to explain the fact that over the centuries most of the Jewish people seem to have failed to embrace Jesus as their Messiah. However, as we have seen throughout this book, on deeper analysis Replacement Theology has brought terrible suffering to the Jewish people over the centuries. It has led Gentile Christians to develop a terrible degree of arrogance, resulting in actions on the part of professing Christians so callous and contrary to the teachings of Jesus that even the most ardent modern advocates of Replacement Theology would repudiate them today.

Most modern supporters of this doctrine would agree with me that the history of the Church and its treatment of the Jewish people has been horrendous. They would claim that the Church leaders had wrongly interpreted this doctrine. They would suggest that it was their misinterpretation of this doctrine, not the doctrine of Replacement Theology itself, which led to the evils of anti-Jewishness that have resulted in such acts of wickedness.

I would argue that these Christian brethren are sincerely wrong in their opinion. Jesus taught that we are to judge spiritual teachings by the kind of fruit that they produce. In Matthew 7:15-20 Jesus warned his disciples regarding the danger of deception by false prophets. He stated that the way to discern the difference between true prophets and false ones was to examine the fruit of their prophetic utterances. True prophets would produce good fruit and false prophets would produce bad fruit. He concluded that by their fruit you would know them. I believe that the same principle should be applied to professing biblical teachers and their teachings. Good fruit will arise from sound biblical teachers and their teaching and equally bad fruit will arise from false teachers and their teaching.

By this principle surely one must reach the conclusion that Replacement Theology has produced the most appalling fruit possible. I would argue that this false teaching is still producing the bad fruit of anti-Jewishness wherever it is taught and believed. The advocates of Replacement Theology seem to have an almost irrational hatred of the State of Israel whilst at the same time attempting to deny that they are anti-Jewish. They accuse Christian Zionists of stirring up hatred against the Arabs and urging the government of Israel to launch wars of conquest against her Arab neighbours. I know of no such Christian Zionists. Those who believe Israel's borders will be extended believe that God will be the agent who brings this about. Most would agree that this will only occur at the second coming of Jesus. Advocates of Replacement Theology are either guilty of deliberately misrepresenting their theological opponents or are genuinely detached from the reality of what is taking place in the Middle East and how most Christian Zionists view these events. At the same time they seem to have a view of the Arab nations surrounding Israel and the Palestinian movements that is so benevolent that they seem to have lost all touch with reality. They seem to be completely unaware of the threat to world peace that militant followers of Islam pose. The poison of Replacement Theology is still leading professing Christians to be inherently anti-Jewish. The poison is still working within the Christian Church.

I believe it is my role, along with all Christian Zionists who are called to be Bible teachers, to oppose the doctrine of Replacement Theology. I believe that in the words the Holy Spirit gave to Jude we are to "contend for the faith once given to the saints" (see Jude:3). Jude wrote his letter to warn his fellow believers in Jesus regarding false teachers that had crept into the Christian Church and were engaging in corrupting and destroying the Church from within. I do not think that these men who were throwing the early Church into considerable confusion set out with the intention of becoming false teachers. I believe that they were genuinely misguided and deceived. I believe that in the same way most, if not all, of the pro-Palestinian theologians are sincere men and women of goodwill that have been deceived concerning the reality of the situation in the Middle East. I believe that they have also been deceived to a large measure as to how the Bible should be interpreted.

The question logically arises as to how we are to contend for the true faith of biblical Christianity. The apostle Paul gives us a very clear answer as to how teachers of the Bible are to seek to correct fellow believers who have been misled. In 2 Timothy 2:24-26 Paul instructs Timothy, a young pastor and teacher, as to how to seek to correct those in the Church who fall prey to false teaching.

Firstly, he warns Timothy not to fall into the trap of becoming quarrelsome. He then advises that Timothy must seek to be gentle and kindly to those whom he seeks to correct. He must at all costs seek to avoid becoming ill-tempered. I believe that we can only minister in this way when we seek to be constantly filled by the Holy Spirit and to be filled with God's love. I believe that we have to ask to see our theological opponents through the eyes of Jesus, which are eyes of compassion. In Revelation 3:18 the risen Jesus asks erring believers at Laodicea to ask of him that he might put a spiritual eye ointment upon their eyes that they might begin to see things the way he sees them.

In the same way, I believe we need to ask Jesus to help us see our theological opponents through his eyes. This cannot come naturally to us. The next thing Paul suggests to Timothy is that he must seek to be skilled in his teaching, for him to know well what we call the Old Testament. Today we teachers need to know our Bibles well and constantly, humbly seek for God to bring the right teaching through our lips. Following this, Paul advises Timothy to seek to correct his opponents with both gentleness and courtesy. I believe that this too is essential advice to all Bible teachers today. He then urges Timothy to look to God to bring about genuine repentance to those whom he has sought to correct. In the same way I believe that we should pray lovingly and humbly for those that have been bound by this false teaching. I am always aware that were it not for God's grace and the sound Bible teachers who taught me, I today might have been bound by this wrong teaching. I believe that this is one way that we can see the love of God working through us as an antidote to the poison in the pot.

During my pastoral ministry I have become all too aware that sometimes people can be intellectually persuaded by the weight of biblical evidence that Replacement Theology is a false teaching, yet still choose to remain anti-Jewish. I once had a lady in the fellowship who seemed to have an unnatural loathing for all things Jewish. Despite this fact she remained in the fellowship which I lead for many months. Her nickname among many of the congregation was 'stage-whisperer'. Whenever I would say anything remotely positive about the Jewish people she would screw up her face and mutter loudly, "Jews again; he's on about Jews again." The congregation simply ignored this behaviour and prayed quietly for her at home.

Surprisingly, she attended a regular weekly church Bible study where I taught Romans chapters 9, 10 and 11. She knew that these chapters were all about the Jewish people but still attended. For a few months her stage-whispers ceased. She seemed a different woman. She asked questions at the end of the Bible study sessions which indicated she was attentively listening to the teaching that I was bringing regarding these chapters. My hopes for a permanent solution to her inherent anti-Jewishness began to rise. Yet I was soon to be disappointed.

When I had completed this study on these chapters this dear sister requested to have a meeting with me and another leader from our fellowship. I could hardly believe the words that proceeded from her mouth. She said that she fully accepted that the Jews had not been rejected from their role as the chosen people. She also accepted the principle that we are all to blame for the death of Jesus since it was the sin of each one of us that caused Jesus to have to surrender himself to death upon the cross. However, she went on to state that she would never ask God to give her his love towards the Jewish people. She even stated that she would always hate the Jews and that she did not want to be delivered from these hateful feelings. She claimed that she now understood why I was so passionate about my mission to eradicate anti-Jewishness from the fellowship and from the wider Christian community. She went on to praise the quality of the vast majority of the things I taught from the Bible. This was high praise indeed from this sister. Then she stated the sad news that she would have to leave the fellowship because she remained out of step with me and the other church members.

Obviously I urged her to think again regarding the issues we had discussed and to pray about her decision as to whether or not she should leave the fellowship. There was an air of sadness about this sister as she spoke to us. She attended one last Sunday morning service with our fellowship. The problem emerged when I simply mentioned the Jewish people in the message that I taught that morning. That was sufficient to inflame her smouldering opposition. She returned to her strategy of stage-whispers to voice her opposition to what I was teaching.

She stated, "He's on about Jews again. It is Jews for breakfast, Jews for lunch and Jews for tea."

She knew that I would have to take serious action about her return to open opposition in such a blatant manner. She knew that I simply could not turn a blind eye to this provocation. I resorted to my rather naughty sense of humour. I stated that despite our sisters' concerns I would not be advocating any form of cannibalism whatsoever. Laughter erupted among the congregation, and a very awkward moment was diffused. Even the offending sister managed to laugh with us. It was her swansong. She thanked me for the good input she had received under my ministry and left for good. I am glad to say that none of the members of the fellowship gloated over her exit from us. Many of our fellowship still pray for this sister to respond to God's love and open the way for the Holy Spirit to set her free from the bondage of her bitterness towards the Jewish people. We realise the fact that God never overrules human free will, so he will not force her to receive healing from this bitterness of spirit.

This example highlights the fact that many who have been entrapped by the doctrine of Replacement Theology need to be set free from a strong delusion by God's healing grace and deliverance. Their abhorrence of all things Jewish is often based on a bitterness of spirit towards the Jewish people. Like the dear sister who accepted that Replacement Theology is unscriptural yet still wanted to hold fast to her abhorrence of all things Jewish, I believe that many Christians who hold to this doctrine do so to justify an inherent anti-Jewishness that they wish to hold on to. I believe that often these Christians do not even understand their feelings. Only the love of God and the inner healing of the Holy Spirit can set these folk free. I believe that other Christians that have been influenced by Replacement Theology can be set free when they come to realise that this teaching is biblically wrong and the dreadful fruit that has arisen from it.

My church secretary, the late Brian Fawcett, was one of these dear Christian believers who came to understand that he had been wrongly influenced by Replacement Theology and sought to be set free from this negative influence upon his life. When he received biblical teaching exposing why Replacement Theology was wrong he completely renounced any negative attitudes towards the Jewish people and the State of Israel. Over a short space of time he developed a tremendous love for the Jewish people and often attended our Prayer for Israel meetings with his dear wife Joan. Brian also introduced me to the value of the internet as he taught me to download positive material supporting the Jewish people from many different websites. Joan remains a very active member of our leadership team. In a similar way Carl, one of our younger members, when he joined the fellowship, was somewhat surprised by the emphasis we place on knowing the Jewishness of our roots in Jesus. However, after a very short while he came to understand the importance of this teaching. During the very first Prayer for Israel meeting he attended he asked for God to give him his love for the Jewish people. He found himself weeping tears of compassion as he felt something of God's heart for them and his sorrow over their bitter persecution over the centuries of Church history. He has grown in his faith in Jesus over the years and now is an active member of our leadership team. This leads me to suggest that in different situations we face we should challenge our fellow believers to ask God to reveal to them whether Replacement Theology is true or false and how he wants them to relate to the Jewish people. I believe that God will always guide people into the right path when they sincerely desire to know his will.

Although I believe that a good knowledge of the Bible regarding the Jewish people is a wonderful blessing to have, it is not the only thing that

God requires of those of us which have received the revelation of God's love for his people. I believe that we all need to ask God to help us to feel his heart for his people, to have his compassion towards them. From the time of my conversion I have had the wonderful experience of being taught by Bible Teachers who have had a revelation of God's love towards the Jewish people. It was only when I studied Theology at university level that I became fully aware of how pervasive the doctrine of Replacement Theology is throughout the Church. It was only as I learned of the appalling litany of crimes committed by professing Christians against the Jewish people that I found myself shedding tears as I interceded for them. Only since then can I claim to have felt something of the sorrow that the God of Israel feels for his people. I believe that we all need to come to this place if we would effectively intercede for the Jewish people in the way that God desires of us.

Only genuine tears shed by the Gentile believers in Jesus will help to heal the terrible, lasting wounds that the professing Church has inflicted upon the Jewish people. It is only these genuine tears that will help non-Messianic Jews to embrace Jesus as their Messiah.

More tears is the urgent need on behalf of the Jewish people and the State of Israel today. More tears must flow from the Church's eyes before tears of repentance, and then tears of joy, will flow from Israel's eyes.[16]

Only when we are filled with God's love and compassion for the Jewish people can we shed these genuine tears of intercession for them. Only deep intercession can help to bring about the wonderful spiritual revival among the Jewish people predicted by Apostle Paul in Romans 11:25-27 and by the prophet Zechariah in Zechariah 12:10-14 and 13:1-2. When we shed tears for the Jewish people we are following the example of Jesus himself that we read of in Matthew 23:37-39. It is amazing to think that Jesus shed these tears at the same time that he was fully aware of the impending ordeal of crucifixion he was about to endure. These tears were not tears for himself, but tears for the Jewish people.

---

[16] Michael Brown

In the same manner, I believe, we need to ask that we might shed tears of intercession for our fellow Christians that have been so deceived by the doctrine of Replacement Theology. Michael Brown draws attention to the sad spiritual state of much of the Church:

But the Church's want of tears for Israel has not only hurt the Jewish people; it has also injured Christians. An unchecked cancer has been running through our ranks, a disease called lack of compassion. Deep repentant love is the only cure.

He compares this lack of compassion in regard to much of the Christian Church to the lack of compassion that existed among the wealthy, self-satisfied, complacent Jewish leaders that were around at the time of the prophet Amos. They were severely judged by God because they failed to grieve over "the ruin of Jacob" (see Amos 6:6). He suggests that this same principle applies to so much of the Christian Church in regard to their terrible lack of compassion for the Jewish people.

Michael Brown writes:

This depicts the Church so well. It is not the persecuted Church that has persecuted the Jews, but the prosperous Church that has hounded them. It is not the humble, broken Church that has robbed God's promises from the Jews, but the arrogant, self-sufficient Church that has stolen them. The Church in its grandeur, the Church in its might, has not grieved over the ruin of Joseph. It has not felt Israel's anguish. Instead, it has mocked the suffering of the Jewish people. In fact, it has contributed greatly to the nightmare of pain.

I believe God is already judging the nations for their attempts to undermine the modern State of Israel and rob the Jews of Jerusalem in the name of promoting peace. In Zechariah 12:1-3 God foretells through his prophet that these actions on the part of the nations will bring down his punishment upon them. I believe that this prophecy is being fulfilled now. The dreadful, almost unprecedented financial crisis gripping the nations, I believe, is taking place because of the actions of the leading nations in regard to Israel. I believe that the most tragic thing that is taking place is the failure of so many influential Church leaders to speak out and warn our politicians of how their actions are bringing God's judgment and punishment upon the nations which they lead.

If this is not the correct interpretation of Zechariah 12:1-3, I ask my readers what is the meaning of these verses? Are the nations that are coming against Jerusalem not rupturing themselves? My prayer is that men and women in high political office will read this book and be challenged by the message it contains. In the same way my prayer is also that my fellow Christian leaders might read this book and be inspired to challenge the complacent Church to seek to show genuine compassion towards the Jewish people and sound out a warning to our national leaders regarding their treatment of them. In this regard I believe that I am not being at all political but biblical. I think it highly hypocritical of some of the proponents of Replacement Theology to accuse Christian Zionists of being too political whilst they themselves are openly supportive of the Palestinian cause. They are not seeking to be fair to both sides in the conflict. They are openly one-sided, openly anti-Israel. They seem to claim that being vehemently anti-Israel does not mean they are anti-Jewish. I fail to perceive the logic of their position. They claim to be the compassionate Christians, the ones who are interested in promoting social justice. Yet they are most uncompassionate towards the Jewish people. I believe that they are most unjust towards the Jewish people in denying them the right to have a homeland with secure borders. They fail to see any danger arising from their forming an alliance with militant Muslims that openly profess to want the destruction of the State of Israel. If a Palestinian State was to replace Israel, would it be a democratic state, permitting the Jewish people to live within it as equals, having the right to vote and the right to free-speech and security? I fear not. I am equally clear that God will not allow this scenario to emerge. The Bible makes it obvious to any sincere student of biblical prophecy that the restored State of Israel will exist up until the second coming of Jesus.

In the last section of this chapter I will suggest some of the ways in which the Christian Church needs to be reformed once Gentile believers take on board God's command to comfort his Jewish people according to Isaiah chapter 40 verses 1 and 2. This will take place once Christian believers ask God to give them his compassion and genuine love for the Jewish people. The first thing that will occur when this takes place is that individual believers and church leaders will shed tears over the way the Church has treated the Jewish people over the centuries; thus the poisonous influence of Replacement Theology will be completely removed from them. Their spiritual eyes will then be opened; hence these believers and church leaders will be able to intercede for the Jewish people and be able to witness in a sympathetic manner to non-Messianic Jews. Organisations like 'Jews for Jesus' are only too willing to help prepare Christian believers to be sympathetic witnesses to the Jewish people. They will also receive from the Lord his enabling to intercede for their fellow believers who have been spiritually blinded by Replacement Theology. They will also begin to appreciate the Jewish roots of our faith in Jesus and to appreciate the actual feasts God commissioned. They will realise that these were the feasts Jesus celebrated with his disciples and that these feasts will be celebrated in God's eternal kingdom when Jesus returns again in glory. When celebrating these feasts it soon becomes apparent that they relate so clearly to Jesus, the Messiah of Israel. Our members have thoroughly enjoyed learning of these feasts and celebrating them over the years. Non-Messianic Jews seem to always be interested in our celebration of their feasts, from my experience of conversing with them.

I always stress the fact that we do so because of the Jewish heritage we have received from them, and I constantly make clear to them my consciousness of the enormous debt we owe to their ancestors as believers in Yeshua (Jesus). They will take on board the fact that the State of Israel has been demonised in the world's media and seek to develop a true understanding of the history of the rebirth of Israel as the fulfilment of biblical prophecy. They will seek to foster a proper unbiased understanding of what is really taking place in the Middle East and pray for genuine peace to be achieved between Jew and Arab. I am not for one moment saying that the government of the State of Israel is perfect and that Christians should praise all that the Israel Defence Forces do. Rather I am suggesting that Christians should oppose bias and misrepresentation regarding the State of Israel. We should pray for more balanced reporting to take place across the world's media. We should also use our democratic rights to oppose political decisions designed to undermine the State of Israel and to scrutinise the decisions of our politicians that will negatively affect the Jewish people. We should also seek to stand up against the wave of anti-Jewishness that is sweeping across much of the western world.

My dear friend, the late Russell Cohen, a dear Messianic Jew, often expressed to me his bewilderment regarding the way that so many Christians are so opposed to the State of Israel. He said that this was a genuine obstacle to him and his fellow Jewish believers whenever they attempted to speak about Jesus to non-Messianic Jews. Russell could never understand why so many Christians failed to perceive the fact that the State of Israel is so vital to the Jewish people as a home where they have a right of return and that its restoration is so clearly the fulfilment of biblical prophecy. We should publicise the fact that when the State of Israel was formed the indigenous Arabs were offered the full rights of citizenship within the new republic. Those that refused to be part of the new state voluntarily left to become exiles. The Arabs that left the new State of Israel believed that the surrounding Arab States would successfully invade the new republic and that they could return to their homes victorious. It was indeed these exiles that form the group that now call themselves the Palestinians. Sadly these historical facts are little known.

One interesting way that my fellowship has of stating our identity as a Christian group that loves and appreciates the Jewish people is to have our Prayer for Israel table prominently displayed. Brian, a member of the fellowship, constantly finds new ways of attractively presenting information about the Jewish people on this table. I often joke with our members about the table acting like a large bunch of garlic bulbs to deter anti-Jewish vampires from joining the fellowship! I am really glad to have this table.

On Saturdays we have held outreach meetings in our nearest city, specifically aimed at challenging Jewish friends with the Messiah-ship of Jesus. We avoid using crosses when endeavouring to witness to non-Messianic Jews. We also avoid words like 'conversion', preferring to talk of Jewish people being fulfilled in their Messiah. After all, religious Jews already worship the God of Israel, as do we as believers in Jesus.

We recognise the fact that Jewish people are free to choose to eat 'kosher' foods. We, as a fellowship, are always prepared to eat only 'kosher' foods with any Jewish friends when they choose to visit us and join us for a meal. In making this provision we are following the advice of the apostle Paul in Romans 14. Whilst opposing Gentiles seeking circumcision for religious reasons, due to the apostle Paul's admonition to the Church in Galatia (see Galatians 5:1-13), I fully accept that some Messianic Jews may choose to circumcise their children according to their own culture as set out in the Law of Moses. This is exactly what Paul encouraged his dear disciple Timothy to do (see Acts 16:1-3). Timothy was born Jewish by virtue of his mother's Jewishness. In order not to give any offence to his fellow Jews, Paul encouraged him to be circumcised. He would have fiercely opposed any of his Gentile co-workers being circumcised for religious reasons.

I seriously believe that as Christians ask to be filled with the love of God, the poison in the pot can be neutralised and church fellowships can be set free from the negative influence that Replacement Theology has had upon its members. Many individual Christian believers can be helped to recognise the fact that they have been deceived by the doctrine of Replacement Theology and become filled by the love of God for his Jewish people. They can become part of what God is doing and will do among these people. Sadly I cannot be completely optimistic about the entire Church. In Matthew chapter 24 Jesus warned that many believers would sadly succumb to the influence of deception. Apostle Paul warned of this same danger in 1 Timothy 4:1-5. Having studied Church history in some depth, seeing the sins of arrogance and intolerance playing such a major role in shaping the Church's past, it hardly gives me great confidence to believe that all professing Christians will unite together to fulfil God's designs for the Jewish people. I believe that it will only be a remnant body of believers that will be free from the influence of deception. Hopefully this will be a very large remnant which God can use to declare to the Jewish people, "Behold your God" (see Isaiah 52:7-11).

I consider it a great privilege to have been able to write this book as a challenge to my fellow believers in Jesus. My prayer is that those who already have a love for the Jewish people will become better equipped in challenging those believers who have either consciously or unconsciously come under the influence of Replacement Theology. I also pray that my book may play a part in helping believers who have been deceived by this poisonous doctrine to be set free from it.

Bibliography

Sources referred to throughout this book:

- The Bible, New International version.
- Zionism and Israel- Encyclopaedic Dictionary.
- Strong's Exhaustive Concordance of the Bible.

Sources referred to in Introduction:

'Continuity and Discontinuity; Perspectives on the Testaments' edited by John Feinberg.
Article: 'Replacement Theology, its Origins, Teaching and Errors' by Dr. Gary Hendrick.
Article: '"Prophets who Prophesy Lies in my Name": Christian Palestinianism and the anti-Israel Crusade' by Dr. Paul Wilkinson

Sources referred to in Chapter 2:

Article: 'How did a nice Jewish Church become Gentile?' by Jim Gerrish. Found in the Church and Israel Forum.
Article: 'Evidence of the Jewish background of the early Church' by Dr. Ron Moseley.

Sources referred to in Chapter 3:

Article: 'Pharisees, Sadducees and Essenes' from the Jewish Virtual Library by Mitchell Bard.
Article taken from The New World Encyclopaedia: 'The Sadducees'.

Source referred to in Chapter 5:

'Roots of our Faith' by Chuck Cohen.

Sources referred to in Chapter 6:

'Our Hands are Stained with Blood' by Michael Brown.
Article: 'Christian hatred and persecution of the Jews' by Phyllis Petty.
Article: 'The Error of Replacement Theology' by Clarence Wagner.
Article: '"Prophets who Prophesy Lies in my Name": Christian
Palestinianism and the Anti-Israel Crusade' by Dr. Paul Wilkinson.
'Zionism and Israel Encyclopaedic Dictionary'.

Sources referred to in Chapter 7:

'Our Hands are Stained with Blood' by Michael Brown.
Article: 'Christian Hatred and Persecution of the Jews' by Phyllis Petty.
Article: 'Martin Luther's Dirty little Book on the Jews and their Lies' by
Jim Walker.

Sources referred to in Chapter 8:

'Our Hands are Stained with Blood' by Michael Brown.
'The Spanish Inquisition' by Rafael Sabatini.
Article: 'Does Israel have a Future?' by Ray Sutton.
Article: 'The Error of Replacement Theology' by Clarence Wagner.

Sources referred to in Chapter 9:

'Our Hands are Stained with Blood' by Michael Brown.
'Christian Zionism: Road to Armageddon' by Dr. Stephen Sizer.
'Christian Zionism' by Derek White.
Article: 'The Error of Replacement Theology' by Clarence Wagner.
Dr. Stephen Sizer as quoted by www.christianzionism.org.
Article: 'Christian Zionism. What are they saying about it?' Taken from the
Wild Olive internet site.

Is there Death in the Pot?

Sources referred to in Chapter 10:

'A Palestinian Cry for Reconciliation' by Naim Ateek.
'Challenging Christian Zionism' by Naim Ateek.
'Justice and only Justice' by Naim Ateek.
'Eurabia' by Bat Ye'or.
'Basic Bible Interpretation' by Roy Zuck.
Article: '"Prophets who Prophesy Lies in my Name": Christian
Palestinianism and the Anti-Israel Crusade' by Dr. Paul Wilkinson.

Sources referred to in Chapter 11:

'For Zion's Sake' by Dr. Howard Morgan.

Sources referred to in Chapter 12:

'Zionism and Israel Encyclopaedic Dictionary'.
'Ours Hands are Stained with Blood' by Michael Brown.
'Christian Zionism Defined' by Mikael Knighton.
John Hagee: as quoted from his website.
Article: 'Lovers of Zion' by Thomas Ice.
Article: 'A Wesley Zionist Hymn' by Herbert McGonigle.

Sources referred to in Chapter 13:

Article: 'Psalm 83 and Islam' by Walid Shoebat.
Website: www.bible411.com

Source referred to in Chapter 14:

'Our Hands are Stained with Blood' by Michael Brown.

From the Publisher

Other titles in the **Timeless Teaching** series:

Books available from the publisher:
www.onwardsandupwards.org